"Victoria's book provides viable strategies, relevant and timely information, as well as practical advice, making this book a powerful antidote to the corrosive affect a career in law enforcement can have on a marriage."

—*Barbara Upham, OEA Sergeant,*
California Highway Patrol

"In her book, *A CHiP on my Shoulder,* Victoria Newman offers a career of practical advice for the emergency responder spouse/partner. The goal of presenting real life issues paired with straightforward thinking and problem solving is reached many times throughout the book."

—*Joel Fay, PsyD, President of West*
Coast Post-Trauma Retreat

"*A CHiP on my Shoulder* is realistic, positive and filled with simple wisdom. Victoria's candid account of life married to a California Highway Patrolman covers a lot of ground. Reading it is like talking with a trusted friend."

—*Ellen Kirschman, PhD, Author of I Love*
a Cop: What Police Families Need to Know

"The foundation of every ethical, competent law enforcement officer is a solid personal life. *A CHiP on my Shoulder* is a survival guide for the police family that functions as a road map to keep that police family solid. The law enforcement landscape tragically is filled with failed marriages and broken families that could have been avoided. Victoria points out how to not become one of those statistics. She shows us that a successful police marriage is not based on whether the two people loved each other at the starting point of their life together, but rather how they live out that love each day. *A CHiP on my Shoulder* gives law enforcement specific insights into the journey. It should be given to the significant others of all police academy graduates as part of their survival training."

—*Kevin M. Gilmartin, PhD, Author of*
Emotional Survival for Law Enforcement:
A Guide for Officers and Their Families

"Life in a law enforcement marriage is sometimes frustrating, sometimes frightening, sometimes a roller coaster thrill ride and often a rewarding personal journey. *A CHiP on my Shoulder* is a warm and insightful glimpse into the challenge of keeping the "shine" on a law enforcement relationship. With tenderness and good humor, Victoria delivers sound advice and words of wisdom that are sure to benefit families of law enforcement personnel, whether they are green-at-the-gills rookies or old-timers trying to figure out 'what happened here?!' A read of this book is a great investment in your law enforcement relationship bank account."

—*Elizabeth Dansie, M.A., B.C.E.T.S.,*
The Psychological Services Group

"From day one of our marriages, we fall into patterns. Patterns we choose or patterns that we simply do because of who we are or where we come from. In a law enforcement marriage, those patterns are intensified, as are almost every other aspect of life in our duty bubble. *A CHiP on my Shoulder* gives the chance to recognize those patterns and evaluate them in a positive way. Brilliant!"

—*Rebecca Qualls, California*
Highway Patrol Wife, 11 years

A wonderful, life saving, life affirming book! Required reading for every cop, and for every cop's spouse, and for all those who love and support our cops.

—*Lt. Col. Dave Grossman, USA (ret.)*
Author of On Combat *and* On Killing

a CHiP
on my shoulder

Lindsey—
Thank you for
your service & sacrifice
as an LEOW!
God Bless—
[signature]

Victoria M. Newman

a CHiP
on my shoulder

HOW TO LOVE YOUR
COP WITH ATTITUDE

TATE PUBLISHING
AND **ENTERPRISES**, LLC

Published by Tate Publishing & Enterprises, LLC
127 E. Trade Center Terrace | Mustang, Oklahoma 73064 USA
1.888.361.9473 | www.tatepublishing.com

Tate Publishing is committed to excellence in the publishing industry. The company reflects the philosophy established by the founders, based on Psalm 68:11,
"The Lord gave the word and great was the company of those who published it."

Book design copyright © 2011 by Tate Publishing, LLC. All rights reserved.
Photography by Donna Shelby
Cover design by Christina Hicks
Interior design by Joel Uber

Published in the United States of America

ISBN: 978-1-61346-592-9
1. Family & Relationships: Marriage
2. Self-Help: Personal Growth, General
11.08.05

Dedication

For the CHiP on my shoulder. Whatever life holds
for us, I'm glad we'll be holding each other.

I love you, Brent.

Acknowledgements

Although there is only one name on the cover, many aspects of this book were put together by a team who adopted my vision and joined my effort in several capacities. I give credit to the following:

My readers: Ginny Yttrup; Teddi Depner; Beth Dansie; Barb Upham; Joel Fay; Michelle Walker; Ellen Kirschman; Mindi Russell; Kevin Gilmartin; Rebecca Qualls; Bernie Homme; Dave Grossman; and my husband, Brent. Each read parts of the manuscript, providing valuable feedback. I appreciate the time and critique they provided. It was exactly what this book needed. Many thanks.

My focus group members (last names withheld to protect their privacy): Kim, Julie, Beth, Stephanie, Maria, Susan, Diana, Erin, Frances, Tricia, Rebecca, Christina, Debbie, Bonnie, Candy, Wendy, and Sandy provided stories, quotes, and input. I also interviewed several others individually and have added their stories as well: Rodney; Clarke; Lori; Emmett; Rachel; Tracy; James; Anna; Barb; Rachel; Chris; and my grandparents, Bernie and Helen. Their support and willingness to speak candidly proved invaluable in my writing and will be a blessing to those who read this book.

I would like to thank Stacy Baker and James Bare from Tate Publishing. They envisioned what this book could be, and lent their encouragement and expertise to make it so. I appreciate their professionalism and candor.

My writer's group—Linda, Barb, Ginny, Tammy, Dee, Rebecca, and Teddi—have allowed me to share my dream and bounce ideas off them for several years now. My thanks to them for journeying with me through tears and laughter.

My support team—Rachel; Mike and Nancy; David and Amanda; Donna; Christina; Rachel; Nancy; Jill; Renee; Kathryn; Kathryn; Lorie; Linda; Rachel; Rebecca; Deb; Barb; Janice; Gary and Mary; Bernie and Helen; Rose; Paula; Annette; Mary; Tammie; Jenny; Sharol; Brent; Dee; Ginny; Bonnie; Fred; Carol; Kris; Barbara and Frances—prayed and encouraged me for months. Thanks to them for many notes, calls, and prayers. They've been my strength and perseverance.

There are several others who put in time to help me when needed. Donna Shelby and Russell and Kira Stevens spent a full (but fun) day contributing to the amazing cover. Kathryn Redman offered excellent marketing direction. Dave and Rose Wertheim lent direction and experience. Barb Upham, Omar Watson and Bernie Homme assisted with my endorsements. And countless others have offered support, ideas and kind words throughout this journey. May God bless you!

I have one supporter who wishes to remain anonymous. This person has been an unexpected blessing to this book and in my life. Many kindnesses were used of God so that every step of this process would come to be. God saved his life, and now he is saving others in return.

My kids—Kyrie, Ben, Annika, and David—have been on this journey with me day by day. They cooked and cleaned, solved problems on their own, and gave me permission to hide out in the office for hours. They listened with interest and provided feedback with hugs and encouragement. They dried my tears and celebrated with me with enthusiasm and love. I appreciate each one of them.

Brent has been incredibly supportive through each step of this entire journey, and I am so thankful for him. He has been willing to speak truth into my life, to be vulnerable on the pages for the sake of other marriages, to offer wisdom in several conversations, and has told many others about the book. I couldn't have done this without him.

Everything I am and will be I owe to Jesus Christ. I thank Him for the call and thank Him for my dream. He will keep leading me, loving me, and changing me. All the credit goes to Him.

Many thanks to each and every one of you!

Foreword

As a Law Enforcement Chaplain for over 20 years, too often I have seen the destruction of marriages between officers and their spouses. It pains me as a minister to the ministers of justice. I can encourage and counsel, but ultimately it is the decision of the couple to have a thriving, long term marriage. In a world where broken people are served by law enforcement officers, I believe this book can be the beginning of renewal. It can help our officers and their families avoid giving up on their life partner and thus becoming another statistic.

As I read *A CHIP on my Shoulder*, two issues were very apparent. First, Victoria has defined the uniqueness of the law enforcement culture. She has shown what it takes to serve and, in turn, what is taken (emotionally, spiritually, physically, and mentally) from these highly committed men and women. They *are* the line between civility and anarchy. She explains the powers and decision-making that no other occupation has: the ability to take away an individual's unalienable rights (life, liberty, and the pursuit of happiness). With just cause, the officer has a profound effect on individual lives, howbeit, settling disputes, investigating accidents and crimes, arresting offenders, testifying in court, aiding the sick, injured, abused, and disturbed, and dealing with all kinds of death. While 96% of law enforcement academies teach officer safety and how to deal with these problems, they don't spend near enough time on *being human,* or in other words, emotional safety. With all of broken humanity, how could they not be affected by the evil they feel, see, hear, touch and smell? How could this pain not transfer to the humanness of our officers? How could this not be a daily assault on their marriages, their well-being, and their perceptions of society?

Secondly, Victoria reveals a truth as a wife: that the best person who can and should stand in the gap for the officer is the spouse. "And the two shall become as one" reminds us that we have to keep both parts healthy. She further explains that the spouse must be just as committed to the *call* as the officer is. Victoria addresses boundaries and expectations of what is normal in this abnormal 24-hour profession. She explains that law enforcement marriages can survive this career and be healthy and happy as well.

For officers who read this book, my prayer is that your emotions will be calmed and your heart will be reminded that you took an oath of commitment and determination to be the best warrior for justice and champion for the innocent you could be. All the sweat and tears in the academy's training paid off. You made it. Great! For officers and spouses, the oath you took as a couple needs that same commitment and determination to prepare for a productive life together.

Read *A CHiP on my Shoulder*. It could be the difference between life and death in your marriage.

—Reverend Master Senior Chaplain
Mindi Russell, Sacramento County, California

Table of Contents

21   **Preface**

23   **Introduction:**
       Attitude Is Everything

27   **Chapter 1:**
       Mr. and Mrs. Cop: What Makes Us Different?

37   **Chapter 2:**
       All Roads, All Codes, All In!

49   **Chapter 3:**
       Creating Your Own Normal

59   **Chapter 4:**
       Code Four Communication

75   **Chapter 5:**
       Game Face: Understanding Your Man

91   **Chapter 6:**
       Thick Skin, Soft Heart: How To Deal Emotionally

107   **Chapter 7:**
        Peeps and Props: Your Support System

123   **Chapter 8:**
        Stuff Happens: When Hard Times Come

147   **Chapter 9:**
        Silver Bullets: Money and Your Marriage

161   **Chapter 10:**
        Little Future Cops

177   **Chapter 11:**
        To Serve and Protect (Your Marriage, That Is!)

205   **Chapter 12:**
        A Seventy Year Vision

211   **Resources**

213   **Endnotes**

Preface

Dear prospective reader,

My husband has served with the California Highway Patrol for over twenty years. The title is attributed to him, as here in California we lovingly refer to our highway patrolmen as CHiPs. However, this book was written for *all* law enforcement wives. I share candidly about my marriage, but the tales told here are not exclusively real stories of the highway patrol. I have done extensive interviews and research to include other departments in and beyond California.

Law enforcement families have many faces. I chose to write this book from my own personal point of view as a woman married to a male officer. This is not meant to exclude those who have a different situation. More than 10 percent of law enforcement officers are women, and there are many non-traditional relationships that make up the law enforcement family community. Many of the principles and ideas I have presented here would be beneficial to all long-term law enforcement relationships.

My hope is that the thoughts and stories shared here will encourage and enrich your marriage to your police officer. I encourage you to talk about these principles with your husband. It could provide an opportunity to talk about areas of law enforcement marriage that you've been unable to figure out. I have also included discussion group questions at the end of each chapter in the event that you get a few wives together and go through the book as a group. It could be the start of some new friendships as you come alongside each other and talk through the issues you share as fellow law enforcement wives.

If you would like further contact with me or want to see more of my writings, please visit my website:

www.how2loveyourcop.com

Enjoy,

Victoria

Introduction:

Attitude Is Everything

"Marriage is hard," he warned. "Marriage to a cop is even harder. You need to think through if you truly want to do this. Do you think you have what it takes to be the few who make it? Most cops are divorced..." The background investigator could tell I wasn't fazed. Which is why he repeated it.

I thought, *How hard could it be? I love him, he loves me. Of course we would make it work.* I didn't really listen because my thoughts were on flowers and white lacy dresses and invitations to our wedding. I thought he was being overly dramatic. I thought he was unnecessarily negative. I wasn't ready to hear how difficult it would be as we embarked on this journey.

So months later, when I found myself in the heart of Los Angeles traffic, scared to death to make a lane change, I remembered his words. I recounted them again when I heard the first heartbreaking stories of people who had taken or ruined lives. They echoed with the sound of a brush hitting the wall during an argument before Brent reported for duty on our first Christmas together. And I remembered his words as I sat on the bed, watching him prepare to enter the LA riots war zone. Slowly but surely, I got an inkling of what Officer Negative was talking about.

I've had a CHiP on my shoulder for over two decades now. We've had a wild and crazy adventure with twists and turns and some seasons I don't care to repeat. Twelve moves, four promotions, and four kids later, I love him more now than in those early days. But that love didn't grow without choosing my attitudes carefully. I'd say this is the key to the success of our marriage and the heart of this book. I consciously made the effort to deal honestly with problems, adopt attitudes that didn't come naturally, and learn to set realistic expectations. It was tough, but I learned to be stronger. So can you.

Along our journey we've been involved in the lives of other policemen and their families. I've interviewed many of them for this book and incorporated their stories, quotes, ideas, and attitudes. In these cases I have changed their names to protect their privacy.

It takes a strong woman to be a cop's wife. We come in all different sizes, shapes, backgrounds, and experiences, but we have a common strength. And that strength is determined by our minds. These pages relate to all of us and can be applied to individual marriages in unique and creative ways. My hope is that these pages will enrich your marriage, helping it to thrive for years to come.

I know a little bit about law enforcement because my father was a police officer. I'd watch him put on his uniform every day. I remember it very well. As a matter of fact, he made me shine his belt buckle and polish his shoes every morning. That part I hated, I have to admit it. But I loved watching him put on his uniform... He always let me put on his jacket first before he put it on. I remember I was so little the jacket went all the way down to the floor... And I watched him put his shield on his chest and walk proudly out of the door. That gave me the deep respect for our law enforcement officers and also for their families... Because I understand what it's like to say goodbye to your loved one each and every day and wonder if this is the day that they do not come home. Is this the day that there will be a knock on the door and our lives would change forever?

Arnold Schwarzenegger
Governor of California
Commencement Address at the California
Highway Patrol Academy
July 9, 2010

Chapter 1:

Mr. and Mrs. Cop: What Makes Us Different?

> I actually am careful about what I wear to bed when he's on duty. Because I never know when another uniform will knock on my door...
> Fran, CHP wife, thirteen years

> How many normal people use words like *trained observer* and *incident* in their conversations?
> Rhonda, CHP wife, eleven years

I didn't sign up for this when I fell in love with my man. Brent was in that place of college indecision when we met. He had just realized that his first choice, the Air Force Academy, was not to be. There was a whole world of opportunity just waiting to be explored! So he looked into medicine and law, and he even considered becoming a pastor. Another choice was the California Highway Patrol. His dad was on the patrol and encouraged him to throw in an application. While we spent time getting to know each other, he was also following up on each step of the hiring process.

Then we got engaged. The first decision we made as a couple was to say yes to the patrol. We set our wedding date five weeks before he was to report to the California Highway Patrol Academy. I had no idea what I was in for. But I had my guy, and that was all that mattered.

In our minds, we committed to the patrol for five years. It was a way for us to grow up, get some life experience for medicine or ministry. But somewhere along the way, we let go of other opportunities. His career had become a calling.

He became a cop.

If you knew your husband before he became a lawman, you probably witnessed a change in him. Maybe you met your man afterward and you knew what you were in for from the beginning. But, either way, we became cop wives and entered into a life that is different than non-cop wives. Because he is in law enforcement, your marriage is different from others. But why?

Who He Is

Every society needs individuals who will step in and uphold the laws that the collective people agreed were necessary for peace. There will always be those who don't want to follow these rules. Some will, at times, go to significant effort to make sure they get their way and then get away with it. Our husbands devote themselves to restoring and keeping the peace these people disrupt. Some call it the thin blue line—the force that stands between order and chaos.

It's a tough position. Because our husbands are protectors of the peace, they have to be on guard at all times in, and sometimes out, of uniform. Their safety is of utmost importance, as is the safety of their loved ones. As a precaution, protections can be put in place to minimize access to themselves and their families.

Protection of Privacy

When Brent and I moved to Los Angeles, we began to pay a small fee every month to keep our names out of the phonebook. Because I grew up in a small town, this was very foreign to me! But it was for our protection. My husband dealt with questionable characters on duty; therefore, revenge was a possibility. One of the protections we put in place was controlling what information was available to the public. This was before the dawn of the Internet.

There are other things we do as well. We don't shout to the world what his occupation is. When we are out and about, we blend in. We keep to ourselves, but Brent is always watching. He sits in strategic spots with his back against a wall, in view of the exits. He will zero in on suspicious behavior and be ready to jump in (or leave), should something go awry. Most of the time, the kids and I aren't even aware of his vigilance.

We choose our friends wisely. Most cops end up hanging out with other cops, mainly because they understand and trust each other. Brent and I have maintained friendships with both cops and non-cops; it seems to keep our lives in balance. We haven't had any issues with this—most of the time. At times his cop mentality has offended others, but, for the most part, non-cop people are fascinated by the stories and ask lots of questions.

Neighbors are a different thing. We can't dictate who lives next door. Depending on the neighborhood, we've both kept quiet, and informed our neighbors that he was law enforcement. At times it has helped others to know who he is, but not everyone is happy about it.

One December night Brent was on the roof, putting up Christmas lights. Suddenly our neighbor pulled up and said that there was a young man dressed in dark clothing on the side of a single lady's home down the street. Brent jumped in the car and went to investigate, finding him hiding in a ravine. He instantly slipped into cop mode, interrogating the kid as to what he was doing. After an hour or so of following the kid home, calling the sheriff, and calming the neighbors' nerves, we went to bed. The next morning we awoke to vandalized Christmas decorations. Of course, we knew exactly who did it. The kid lived in a rental the next street over, so we held a neighborhood watch meeting, contacted the owner, and by Christmas they were gone. Wouldn't you know? A string of petty thefts in the area ended at the exact same time.

Victoria M. Newman

Stress

Perhaps the biggest impact on your marriage will be the stress of your hubby's job. There are so many pressures on policemen. There's the hatred from criminals, office politics, accusations from the media, a lack of justice in the court systems, armchair second guessing, the heartbreaking injuries and deaths of innocent people, and even uneasiness of law-abiding citizens. It will, at times, affect him in his off time.

Your husband also undergoes physical stress. Not only does he need to rely on his training to get him out of some tight spots, but he also is required to work different shifts that aren't conducive to good sleep. On top of that, he may have trouble eating well, as many times they buy fat-laden fast food to sustain them during long hours (we've heard the donut jokes ad nauseum). Our guys can also be susceptible to injuries or illnesses related to the job, and, of course, this will affect you.

Lastly, there are strong emotions that come with his job. He's been trained to be in control, to bring calm to stormy situations. Most will obey his orders, and the ones who don't may only respond to force. Sometimes it's hard to turn that off when he gets home. What if you and the kids don't adhere to something he wants or asks you to do? When your cop has strong emotions, both in control and out of control, that can affect your relationship and home.

Shift Work/Surveillance

Perhaps one of the most obvious things that set us apart from other marriages is the hours our guys work. Their jobs are driven by emergencies, and we never know what will happen and when. No matter what agency he works for, the hours can be long and unpredictable. Crime and accidents happen twenty-four-seven.

Brenna's husband, Scott, is on the SWAT team for the sheriff's department. He constantly gets calls to report for potential situations. At the onset of one recent incident, he kissed his family goodbye, saying he'd probably be home within the hour. It became a three-day hostage showdown. Scott came home a couple times to get some sleep and then returned. For Brenna and her children, it was the most difficult ordeal they'd experienced thus far. Their lives revolved around *the situation.* Family and friends called constantly for updates, Scott was in high gear the entire time, and it was covered in full-color detail on television.

In addition to long hours, in recent history we have endured something else—deployment. Natural disasters, 9/11, riots, and fires have taken our men to other places to help out local law enforcement in crisis situations. Many policemen are former military, so some cop wives have experience with this. It doesn't make it any easier—and we're left to hold down the fort.

Risk

I remember the news footage from September 11, 2001. There were people of all shapes, sizes, ages, and colors fleeing a wall of dusty debris, leaving shoes, purses, and hats behind. My stomach curdled when I realized what happened. I thought about all the emergency personnel who were in the thick of where that debris was coming from. We lost many good men and women that day.

September 11 serves as a vivid reminder that what our husbands do is dangerous. When everyone else is running *from* danger, they run *to* it. And we know full well the risk that they may not be the same when they return, if they return.

Over the years I've been to my share of law enforcement funerals. I've had widows and family members cry on my shoulder. We have a fallen officer who is buried within a mile of our home, and we visit his grave every year around Thanksgiving, the time of year he died. The risks are real. And the fear that this could happen to us can wreak havoc if not dealt with.

If you've been married to a cop for very long, I'm not telling you anything new. You've already come up with coping mechanisms and solutions to all of these issues. Sometimes all we need is to know that there are others who are experiencing the same thing, and we are bonded through the experience. But whatever stage you are in, dealing with these obstacles begins and ends in your mind.

A Battle for Your Mind

It was a beautiful morning but hot. A small group of men sat in chairs, facing us from the front, their duty uniforms blending in with the helicopters parked behind them. We were honored to be in their presence as the master of ceremonies recounted the heroics of these men while deployed in Afghanistan. Their ordeal sounded like a scene in a movie, but what they'd been through was very real. After they were awarded their distinguished medals, the families joined them up front for pictures. The officer we were there to support was joined only by his kids, as he was divorced.

I felt a lump in my throat. This brave yet humble man before us had been deployed twice to provide medical assistance to those fighting for our freedoms. When at home he serves as a police officer. I'm sure it was very difficult for his wife to endure the loneliness, the risks, and other things that make marriage to a soldier/cop challenging.

Being the wife of a policeman, agent, deputy, or soldier is tough, and there are those who don't make it. I'd like to tell you it's not that difficult, but the facts speak for themselves. Divorce is a very real problem for law enforcement. But it isn't inevitable. Ellen Kirschman, PhD, a clinical psychologist who works with law enforcement and author of *I Love a Cop*, says this: "Several police-specific studies suggest that the first three years of marriage are the most precarious and that if a male officer stays married beyond those

Victoria M. Newman

three years, his marriage is, in fact, more stable than one in the general population."[1]

Sherry agrees with this. The third year of her marriage to her police officer was very difficult. Her husband couldn't juggle the new demands of his job, and they had been struggling for a couple of years. Both sides of their extended family were not familiar with the difficulties facing them as a new law enforcement couple and therefore didn't understand. Finally Sherry moved out. It got everyone's attention. Their relatives rallied around them, and after six months of processing and healing, they reunited. They are now enjoying a thriving marriage of eleven years.

Making the choice to stay or leave starts in the mind. When things are tough, there is a natural tendency to run. When hard times stay for a particularly long season, some women reach their breaking point. They need relief. And there are those who seek relief in leaving. But in many circumstances, divorce is the beginning of a whole new set of problems.

I've had my own mind battles. There are times in my marriage that the vow I pledged back in 1988 was the only thing holding me in place. I will go into this later on. But first let's take a look at the foundation of marriage: commitment.

Discussion Group Questions

1. Was your husband a police officer when you met? If yes, what were your impressions of his job? If no, what is the biggest change you saw in him when he became an officer?

2. Share one of your favorite on-duty stories your husband has told you.

3. What is the most difficult aspect of your husband's job that you struggle with?

4. What are some things you've done in your marriage that have helped with some of these struggles mentioned here?

Chapter 2:
All Roads, All Codes, All In!

Get In, Sit Down, Shut Up and Hang On!
License plate frame, California

It was Christmas Day when I realized our honeymoon was over. I hated our new apartment, I didn't know a soul, and I commuted to work an hour and a half each way through Los Angeles traffic. This place was very different from the small town of Chico where I grew up. On top of that, we had no money, a Charlie Brown Christmas tree we bought for eight bucks at a hardware store, and one gift from my grandparents. Brent was learning his new job in a difficult part of LA, and he worked swing shift on Christmas Eve. Me? Except for the manager's kids who came by to sing carols at my door, I spent it alone.

Earlier in December Brent graduated from the California Highway Patrol Academy, which was then and remains a residential training academy. We were given a week to move downstate and get settled before he reported for duty as a rookie officer in LA. Our six-month marriage was already experiencing a tough season.

We went from five months of weekend-only bliss to shift work and mandatory overtime. We left a small town of supportive family and friends to join a sea of unfamiliar faces and places. Our rent went up significantly, gas became a greater burden, and I had to work full time to make ends meet. We didn't know anyone except other new officers in the same boat. This was hard to handle all at once. But something else bothered me: Brent seemed to be changing, and not for the better.

Working on the streets of LA was affecting him. Brent had been a pre-med student and a church intern when I met him. He was tender and idealistic, but after he became a cop, he turned tough and painfully realistic. He saw some really disturbing things and couldn't share everything with me. His sweet demeanor was disappearing, and I didn't know what to do.

Suspecting I wasn't alone, I gingerly approached another newlywed wife whose husband graduated with Brent.

"Have you noticed a change in Bill lately?" I asked.

"What do you mean?" she replied.

"Well, it's hard to explain. Brent has kind of an edginess now that I haven't seen before. Some language too. He seems frustrated and angry. Has Bill acted like this?"

She looked at me like I was purple and promptly shook her head. I walked away, sorry I ever mentioned it. *Well, that was helpful*, I thought to myself, embarrassed I'd made something out of nothing.

Victoria M. Newman

Three weeks later I was stunned to learn this same gal returned to her mother's home and filed for divorce. Obviously something was wrong, and she chose to shut up and get out. I wasn't giving in so easily. I decided at that moment that I would hold on tight to my man and find help.

But help was hard to find. It seemed everyone was tight-lipped about their relationships. And many of Brent's friends on the patrol were single. So I had to figure it out for myself.

I wondered what I'd gotten myself into. Suddenly I was married to someone different, and it wasn't what I had envisioned. But the one thing that carried me through this early season was the fact that I'd made a promise to Brent in front of God and everyone that I'd stay with him until "death do us part." I had to make it work.

Commit to Your Marriage

Every time I visit the grocery store, I'm reminded how easily promises are made and broken in relationships. While I am putting my food items on the conveyor belt, my eye is drawn to the magazines for the latest Hollywood gossip. This couple is history. That actor dumped his actress lover for another. Secret sexual trysts. Some of these people change partners as often as they change clothes.

I assume that not all of it is true. I understand that the drama is what gets the press. And I know that much of the world doesn't hold the same values as these people. But because of the inundation of careless disregard for commitment that permeates our culture, we can't help but be influenced by it in our thinking. When a marriage experiences tough times, there are some who turn to other options way too soon.

Our wedding day was perfect. But two days before, we had the biggest fight we've had in our entire relationship. Brent and I spent several hours working through a fundamental issue that drew in several people in our wedding party. Looking back, I suppose we could've called it off. But we didn't. Because our minds were already geared that we were in it for keeps, we took the time to wrestle through the drama and get down to the core issue. After the tears dried, we were freed up to thoroughly enjoy our wedding and honeymoon. Even though we were very young, we understood "for better or worse."

True and unwavering commitment requires a purposeful steeling of the mind. It's an attitude that doesn't consider divorce an option. And it is the glue that will hold a couple together through the messiest of times.

The Escape Clause

It doesn't matter how awesome your guy is; there will be a time when your mind will be tempted to entertain other options. Boredom, loneliness, a grass-is-greener moment, another handsome uniform—there are lots of temptations that come along that threaten your

Victoria M. Newman

marital commitment. If your mind isn't engaged for the long-haul, it could get you into trouble.

When I married Brent, I gave my whole heart to him. Or so I thought. A year or two into our marriage, I realized that there was a little spot inside me that I reserved for the "what if." What if he is killed on duty? What if he leaves me for someone else? These were fears that I held in the back of my mind. For a time, I developed a place to retreat to in my mind, just in case these fears came to life. I call this protective inner wall the escape clause. And when things got a little tough, I'd retreat behind that wall and let my mind wander. I'd put together a plan. Where I'd go, how I'd react, and, sometimes, whom I'd consider dating if Brent were gone. Eventually I challenged myself to stay away from the escape clause; it made my commitment waver. And when things got more difficult, I didn't need the temptation to run.

The escape clause has to be taken in context. I am referring to secret thoughts of a woman that are meant to protect but actually hinder her from commitment and complete intimacy. These thoughts are based on a fear of being hurt. By no means am I referring to a relationship in which the husband is abusing his wife emotionally, physically, or sexually. In these situations, there are cases in which separation can actually save a marriage.

Buckle Up

Are you all in? Or will you balk when hard times put you to the test? Are you willing to take courageous, proactive steps to nurture that commitment? I will talk more about these steps in Chapter 11, but for now fasten your seatbelt!

Your seatbelt of commitment, that is. A seatbelt is protection we depend on every time we get in the car. It may seem a bit confining or claustrophobic to some, but it's necessary. Our husbands can attest to accidents they've seen that, had the victims worn seatbelts, they would've been a lot better off. In many cases it is the difference between life and death. When trouble comes, it is the one thing that holds us in place when all else is sliding every which way. In like manner, commitment does the very same thing.

But you have to choose to put it on ahead of time. Trying to do so at the moment of impact is impossible. It's too late.

Commit to the Job

Before your husband was allowed to pin his badge on his uniform, he had to swear an oath to protect and to serve the people of his jurisdiction. Here are a couple examples:

> I will support and defend the Constitution of the United States against all enemies, foreign and domestic; that I will bear true faith and

allegiance to the same; that I take this obligation freely, without any mental reservation or purpose of evasion; and that I will well and faithfully discharge the duties of the office on which I am about to enter. So help me God.

FBI[2]

To serve the United States of America and the State of California honestly, and conscientiously; and fulfill my oath as a soldier of the law; To uphold and maintain the honor and integrity of the California Highway Patrol; Be loyal to my fellow officers; respect and obey my seniors in rank; and enforce the law without fear, favor, or discrimination; Assist those in peril or distress, and, if necessary, lay down my life rather than swerve from the path of duty; My personal conduct shall at all times be above reproach and I will never knowingly commit any act that will in any way bring discredit upon the California Highway Patrol or any member thereof; To all of this I do solemnly pledge my sacred honor as an Officer of the California Highway Patrol.

CHP[3]

The oath your husband swore as a peace officer affects you whether you like it or not. At times this oath will take precedence over things that are very important to you—birthday parties, family dinners, and holidays, to name a few. And it's easy to resent your husband's job when a couple of missed events stack up. This oath can be a foe, or, with the right mindset, it can be a friend. At the very least, we can make peace with it.

It's your choice. When he's running "all roads, all codes" with his hair on fire, will you commit yourself to accept not only the benefits of his job but also the consequences? I may be sounding a bit like Officer Negative (see "Introduction"), but he was right; marriage *is* hard. Being a cop's wife is even harder. But what does commitment look like?

To commit to his job means choosing a good attitude when he's at the jail late and you have to put the kids to bed by yourself. It means talking out your frustrations with him at an appropriate time instead of as he's heading out the door for his shift. It is knowing full well that it may have to be this way until he catches that thief or arrests that killer. It means slipping into survival mode for a time to make things work. It may mean growing up a bit, having your own needs take a back seat to the pressing issues of his job for a time. But then, at the appropriate occasion, voice your concerns courageously instead of stuffing them inside to fester. Committing to his job means knowing that seasons come and go, persevering, and looking forward. This is tough to do and will take some practice, so let me give you one more perspective on this.

Partners at Home

Shortly after I started writing this book, word was spreading about what I was doing. I got a phone call one morning from a sergeant in our employee assistance unit with her full support. She told me that the timing was right for my book, as "the face of law enforcement is changing. We are discovering more and more the importance of emotional care for our officers, and we're doing something about it. The families are a big component of that."

My husband and I knew this early on in our marriage. He told me from the beginning that he couldn't do this without me. I believed it then and even more so now. Your guy can go through the academy, he can train, and he can save lives, but there is another side of him that really needs you. Your respect can bolster his confidence. Your support can give him that extra emotional stability that he will need as his job wears him down. Your love can break down the walls he'll be tempted to build around himself when what he sees hurts his sense of how the world should be. It may seem a little overstated to some, but when I say you are a not-so-silent partner behind the badge, our everyday reality shows it to be true.

Understanding your role in the big picture here can help you deal with the negative pieces of his job and convince you to commit to the cause. There is something to be said about the satisfaction in being a part of something bigger than yourself.

Commit to the Adventure

Solemn commitments are there for the long haul, put in place for the protection of you, your husband, and your marriage. But there are many seasons of pure enjoyment and fulfillment! There are many positive things about being the wife of a police officer. I chose a long time ago to look at our life together as an adventure. I chose a life of ups and downs, twists and turns, highs, lows, and everything in between. And I love it!

Let me share a few of our memories over the years:

I remember turning beat red when a large group of cadets sang "Happy Birthday" to me on the steps of our state capitol. That was definitely cool.

We missed a wedding in Northern California and drove all night to SoCal when Brent decided to return to help with the LA riots even though we were on vacation. Somehow I felt his call of duty and chose to answer it with my full support. There's a satisfaction I have when I recount it now, like I did the right thing for the greater good. Maybe you understand?

When it was time to move, I accepted it, looking forward to a new adventure, and kept in touch with those we left behind. Now I have friends in several parts of the state, and I've never regretted it.

I cried when a twenty-year-old killed her two best friends when she decided to drive drunk.

I laugh as I remember how a poker game in the backyard became a little more eventful when a mole chose to run through a crowd of cigar-smoking cops. There was one less pest in the world to dig up our lawn!

Victoria M. Newman

When my two-year-old son burned his hands after falling into a campfire, Brent's coworkers put together a basket of goodies for him to pass the time with while he healed. The support of other officers and office personnel has been huge when hard times hit.

When a call came in of a nearby pursuit while having a deep conversation at home with out-of-state friends, I quickly helped Brent climb into his uniform and watched him screech away (he was the on-call supervisor). Our friends and I later listened with wild anticipation as he recounted how the pursuit ended in a field of flames with the suspect in custody. Hoorah!

I clapped as tears filled my eyes when I witnessed an incredible victory over tragedy. Months after one of our officers became a paraplegic when he was hit on duty, he hand-pedaled his specialized bike as he joined my husband and his cadets on a run to our state capitol.

I enjoyed being in the know when my husband got to be involved in a high-profile case. He was the first officer on the scene of the burned-out car that belonged to the victims of the highly publicized Yosemite murders.

These are just a few of our memories. You will have your own list if you don't already. From time to time, it feels good to recount the ups and downs like I've done here. It bolsters confidence, knowing that we survived the downs intact, maybe even coming away with a little more strength, a little more wisdom. The ups invite an attitude of thankfulness, enjoying the good times once again.

It's a wild and crazy adventure, a very full life. And know that more great things will be added in the years to come. Commit to the adventure; you'll be glad you did.

Discussion Group Questions

1. What is it that you like about your husband's job?

2. What are some memorable moments from his career that come to mind?

3. How do you feel about being a not-so-silent partner behind the badge?

4. Do you struggle with the escape clause? Elaborate.

5. Which of the three commitments do you need help in? What is one way you can improve?

Chapter 3:

Creating Your Own Normal

I think you have to kinda let go of the life that you thought you were gonna have when you marry an officer. I really do. I think you have to realize that you are in a new life now. And it's gonna throw you curves. It's different than any other job there is out there.

Jenny, former dispatcher and CHP wife

True contentment is a real, even and active virtue—not only affirmative but creative. It is the power of getting out of any situation all there is in it.

G. K. Chesterton

There is no normal. Not really. Gone are the days where we compare ourselves to the Cleavers or the Joneses. We are a creative people collectively. If you took a survey of the households on your street, you might find that someone comes or goes all twenty-four hours of the day. Living in the city, I am always amazed how many people are out and about at four in the morning.

We create our own normal. My normal may be vastly different from your normal. The challenge comes when we try to make plans with others or even those within our own household. With three teenagers in our home, dinners around the table with everyone present are rare. Sports and work schedules prohibit many nights together. When they were smaller, the kids and I had dinner together every night, and normal was either Brent was there, or we kept a plate heated for later. In both situations everyone appreciates when we do have everyone present, and it's usually a really fun night.

Before Brent and I had children, he worked swings (1400 to 2300, military time), and I worked at an office (0800 to 1700). We each were alone for several hours— he in the morning, I in the evening. We chose to look at it positively; we got to see each other at least four days a week. And we took advantage of those moments together and apart. We created our own normal.

DeAnn and Shawn both work and have two busy children. Their lives are very full with so many schedules to juggle. It was quickly becoming unmanageable, so DeAnn bought a whiteboard to put on the wall in the kitchen. Everyone's schedule was placed on the calendar. It was Shawn's responsibility to get his work schedule on the whiteboard in a timely manner. From then on, she was able to be organized and keep the details of the family straight.

I keep two calendars. A large desktop calendar works the best for me; the kids can write in their events and check on dates themselves. Brent, however, uses his Blackberry for his schedule. After several conflicts in communication, Brent asked if I could sync our computers by inputting events on his Gmail calendar. It works perfectly as long as I input things in a timely manner!

Balancing Home Life and Career(s)

Jenny and Tim had been married double-digit years when they had their first child. Before this time she was a dispatcher and he an officer. They worked out their shifts together, and it was relatively easy, considering it was just the two of them. But when their daughter came, things changed. Jenny quit her job to stay home. Tim was still working long hours, and there were other demands that had to be taken care of as well.

In response they set up an agreement. They decided that when he had his days off, he was to give them one full day. The other days were up for grabs, but one day was to be spent with his girls. This worked as they scheduled several days a month to be together.

Kathy and Jerry did something similar. Jerry would come home from long hours on the job and retreat to the computer. He was really good at Farmville, an easy game on Facebook that he used as his down time. But it was creating resentment in Kathy. He'd already been gone for many hours; why would he want to spend more time without her and their son? She came to understand that he, in fact, craved that down time; he needed to think through the demands he felt during his shift. But this understanding didn't entirely solve their problem. What did work was scheduling time to sit together and talk without other distractions. Sometimes they'd talk about their days, other times they got into deep issues, and other times they planned special trips. And occasionally these nice little talks led to intimacy in the bedroom.

Seasons: Recreating Normal

As the years progress, seasons come and go. Seasons of long hours. Seasons of illness. Seasons with children. Seasons with inadequate leadership within the department. Some of these seasons are amazing and some are excruciating. But they come and they go. When we live day to day, it's very easy to forget this.

I took a walk with a physical trainer several years ago. Kate was bemoaning the fact that she was to have surgery on her knee within the week. She was weary of her injury. She was worried about gaining weight and possibly losing her job. She was sure that life would crumble around her and never be the same.

I suggested that she was in a winter season. I explained that there are seasons of life that seem bleak. Colorless. Like there's no hope. She perked up when I told her that winter seasons eventually move into spring seasons. Seasons that show promise of beauty and color. There's newness everywhere, and we get excited in our anticipation. Spring seasons move into

Victoria M. Newman

summer seasons, and so on. Kate told me she'd never heard that before but seemed hopeful. Two months later she led our water aerobics class in a full-hour workout. Spring had come.

It's all about attitude.

If your husband is working really long hours because of a case he's on, it will end at some point. Some seasons are longer than others, but they do change. Your attitude makes the difference. Understand that you have to create a new normal for each season. Adjust expectations. Hold onto hope. Hunker down and persevere during the winter, knowing that spring is on it's way.

Sometimes You Just Have To Be Brave

The laughter was deafening. Emily found herself laughing along; although because she didn't really know these people, she felt a touch uncomfortable. Clara had just opened her white-elephant gift: a set of five condoms. It was definitely appropriate for the crowd. They were all recently married, and everyone's husband or wife was present. That is, everyone's spouse but Emily's. Emily's husband was on duty.

It was her turn. She looked over the gifts that were beautifully wrapped underneath the tree. She chose a gorgeous red box tied with a silver bow. As she started to poke at the ribbon, she thought she heard a guy whisper, "Oh, no." Too late!

At first when Emily opened the box, she had no idea what it was. She lifted it out, and, of course, everyone howled. "What *is* this?" she asked.

Her face flushed crimson as she heard someone shout, "Edible underwear!"

Sometimes you just have to be brave. When events come up, and your husband is working, go. You never know what that event may hold! There will be times when your loneliness will increase because you really wish he was there. But, more often than not, you'll make a memory. Or laugh trying. Sometimes you'll even gain a new friend.

When Brent was a cadet in the academy, I drove home after visiting him in Sacramento. It was very dark, and I was on a stretch of rural highway in the middle of nowhere. Suddenly my car sputtered, coughed, jerked a few times, and I found myself rolling, powerless, to the side of the road. Annoyed, I got out of the car, went around to the front, and froze. I saw small flames flickering underneath. In a panic I lost all sense of safety and waved my arms at a few cars that came by. Finally a young man stopped, put out the fire with some water he had in his car, and assured me everything was okay. There was a spooky-looking house several yards away, and about that time, a flashlight approached. "Do ya need to use a phone?" the creepy resident asked. I flashed a look of fear to the young man, and he accompanied me into the house while I called a tow truck and family. An hour later I was on my way home.

Victoria M. Newman

This was the first time I had to solve a problem like this all by myself. It was scary! Brent was unavailable, my dad was out of town, and I had to grow up and deal. It was good for me. Since that night I can't tell you how many times I've had to take care of problems on my own: hospital visits, car repairs, issues with teachers, landlords, and tenants, you name it. Brent helps me when he can, but, for the most part, I've learned I can hold down the fort quite well.

It would be easy to resent situations like these. It would be easy to resent him for not being there. But a sense of survival or duty can take over if you allow it. In fact, you can even choose to gain a sense of accomplishment from learning new skills. This is the kind of strength we can use to build our new normal.

A word of caution here: We married rescuers. Our guys want to be needed. We must keep this in mind, making sure that we don't become so independent that we cease to need them. I'm talking about balance here, and there is no formula. We have to figure this out with our spouses. Interdependence is the goal, but when our cops aren't able to do something, we have to pick up the slack.

Make It Work!

Christmas doesn't have to be celebrated Christmas morning. The Fourth of July picnic can be on the third, and you'll enjoy it more with less people around!

Vacations don't have to be in the summer months. And days off don't have to be on Saturday and Sunday.

Vacations, holidays, and schedules are yours to tweak to make it work. Each season of your life will have additional considerations. But if you're willing to think outside the box, you'll be surprised how well events turn out.

Brent always liked to work Christmas Eve. It was generally quiet, so he'd have the guys who didn't have families nearby come to the house even if we had other guests. He asked me to "work my magic" in the kitchen and spoil them with flavor. I loved every minute of it. We have very fond memories of candles from the table casting a warm glow on their badges. And there was always laughter with a cop at the table.

Expectations

If you expect that your life is supposed to look like your dad's office job, you will be disappointed. If you expect your husband to make every single event you plan and on time, you will be disappointed. If you don't try to be creative in making memories that include your husband, you will be disappointed. If you refuse to solve some of the problems that arise when he's on duty, you'll have trouble.

The attitude of strength here is flexibility. Creating your own normal and recreating normal are an integral part of a long-lasting law-enforcement marriage. Choosing to be flexible and optimistic in the face of unmet expectations is tough at times but necessary. Managing those expectations with flexibility and optimism ahead of time is even better. Communicating those expectations is another matter altogether.

Discussion Group Questions

1. What does normal look like in your family right now?

2. Name one idea that you came up with to incorporate your husband's job with your family time.

3. What was one expectation you came into your marriage with that didn't pan out?

4. Share about a winter experience and what spring looked like.

Chapter 4:

Code Four Communication

They say marriages are made in heaven. But so
are thunder and lightening.

Clint Eastwood

Words of comfort, skillfully administered, are
the oldest therapy known to man.

Louis Nizer

A sleek, black Lexus caught my eye in the next lane.
Wow. It was shiny and new, and the sun hit it just
right. It's a good thing I noticed it because all of a sud-
den it cut me off! So I'm driving behind this gorgeous
car, and I veered into the left turning lane (with my
signal on). Again, this Lexus cut me off to do the same
(but without a signal). What?! Am I supposed to know
where he's going?!

As we both made the left turn, he made a quick
right into a gas station, once again with no signal.
Because I'd kept my distance for my own car's sake, it
wasn't dramatic, but it made me mad. Such a beautiful
vehicle but the driver was clueless!

I call this "driving on the inside of the car," and it's one of my biggest pet peeves. There are many of these people on the road—those who don't think to let others know what they're doing by flipping a simple switch. (Actually, when I think about it, it really shouldn't bug me. It is, after all, job security for my husband! But I digress…)

It's called a failure to communicate. And it doesn't just happen on the road. It happens in relationships every day. Someone is acting on the thoughts inside her head, and she expects others to be able to understand exactly what she's doing and why. But if she doesn't give out the proper signals, she runs the risk of making someone angry or, worse, causing damage to herself and others.

Lost in Translation

Communication can be so tricky at times. Words come from deep within a person's soul and heart. They come with a set of values, experiences, and personal makeup. On the other end, the same words are received into a new set of values, experiences, and different personal makeup. At times I speak a different language from my husband. I can speak a different language from my kids, my mother-in-law, or fill in the blank.

Much of our communication gets lost in translation. If good communication is critical for a lasting relationship, how can we learn to speak each other's language?

The most obvious way is to spend time with each other. That's a no brainer. But what about when things change, like when a child is born or a critical incident occurs? What about when time goes by, you lose touch, and suddenly you are clueless to what's going on with your husband?

Colorful Personalities

Brent and I had reached a point in our marriage where we were in a rut, struggling to understand each other. We were clashing, not in sync, and we were both frustrated. Then Brent brought home a book called *The Delicate Art of Dancing with Porcupines*, by Bob Phillips. This book is based on four types of people— the analytical, the driver, the expressive, and the amiable— and explores how these people interact and communicate.[4] We answered the questions in the book and were amazed at the results.

When I understood the natural tendencies of my husband, it was a huge "aha" moment and vice versa. We spent a couple of hours laughing over each other's tendencies and how we differ. It gave us freedom to be ourselves and a non-threatening way to give each other the freedom to be who we are. It was a huge step toward understanding each other, and our relationship has only gotten better because of it. When we come to a situation from two different sides, we are able to see where each other is coming from and then come to a better solution for both.

We also learned about a similar program through our church that was adapted from several sources. This tool categorizes people into colors based on personalities. Red people love fun and are very talkative. Blue people tend to be caretakers, romantic, cooperative, and peacemakers. Green people are problem solvers, leaders, and logical in their thinking. Yellow people are planners, punctual, and structured. We became more self-aware and learned how our colors respond to each other.

Brent is a green, and I am a blue-red combo. Bring our kids into the mix and we have all four colors represented. In moments of peace, we all actually talk about what colors we are. It helps to understand why we do what we do and react how we react. It is a valuable tool to step outside of ourselves and see each other with different eyes.

The Man-Woman Thing

I like to joke that when God took a rib from Adam to make Eve, He took a whole lot more than just a bone. He also took the multitasking gene, the tendency to nurture, and the ability to ask for directions! But seriously, not only do we deal with our differences in personalities, we also have the man-woman thing.

So many people are irritated with the obvious differences between males and females. I've seen a lot of women try to change their guys, make an attempt to get them in touch with their feminine side. Men seem to either joke or just shake their heads at female tendencies. It is almost impossible to truly understand the inner workings of the opposite sex. It's a fact: we are different! So how can we live together in harmony?

I say accept the differences and learn to appreciate them. Be who you are as a woman. Let him be who he is as a man. Accept the fact that he can't say as many words as you do in a day and find other outlets (like other females) for the rest of your important thoughts and ideas. Celebrate his ability to be firm with the kids when you waver, and celebrate that you want to hug your little sweetie for as long as she needs. Understand that the best way to talk to your guy is when you do something together. Women like to talk face to face, but men talk best side by side.

We were made to work together. Like a key fits into a lock, our physical anatomy is definitely suited to each other. But it doesn't end with anatomy. Our personality traits, strengths, and natural tendencies are so different it seems for some that we could never be compatible. But with the right attitude and enough time, you and your husband can learn to ebb and flow with each other's strengths and weaknesses. It is a beautiful thing to behold a couple with this kind of balance.

Love Languages

"I just don't feel loved by my husband…" I have heard this from many women throughout the years. Usually her husband actually loves her deeply but isn't able to show her in the way she can receive it. This too is about speaking a different language. In Gary Chapman's book *The 5 Love Languages: The Secret to Love that Lasts*, he describes five ways in which people feel loved. They are quality time, gifts, words of affirmation, physical touch, and acts of service. Each person has at least one of these ways they feel loved, and they tend to show love this way as well. A problem arises when both spouses have different love languages. More often than not, this is the case.

Say that Sue's love language is words of affirmation, and Raymond's is acts of service. Sue will naturally tell Raymond she loves him often, but he would feel more loved if she offered to take his uniforms to the dry cleaners. Raymond will show Sue he loves her by washing her car, but she wants to hear how he loves her and why. Do you get the rub?

Just knowing how to speak each other's love language can improve your communication dramatically. It takes a choice on two fronts: choose to show love in his language, and recognize his love language toward you and appreciate it. Better yet, get proactive; talk about love languages together and use the knowledge to love each other more effectively.

Go Easy; It Takes Time

I once heard a couple who had been married for over forty years say, "We didn't really get each other until we'd gotten the first twenty years out of the way." Now that

Brent and I have been married over twenty-three years, I understand what they were talking about. Entwining two lives into one takes time and patience. It takes being lifelong students of one another. And as soon as you think you have him all figured out, he'll change. So will you. It's the adventure, and it's never dull!

This reminds me of good ol' Shrek and his conversation with Donkey. Shrek refers to himself as an onion. He has layers—really rough on the outside and soft and pliable on the inside. I can look back now and see that our marriage has been like this. We dealt with rough, unattractive stuff early on in our marriage, then, year after year, we continue to enjoy the good stuff.

A Tactical Approach: Communication Killers and Keepers

Learning to speak each other's language is a lifelong pursuit. It's the big picture, a little something to keep in the back of your mind year to year. But what about day to day? That's where the bulk of our communication lies.

There are behaviors and mindsets that will kill the ability to communicate, and there are attitudes and boundaries that will keep the communication flowing. Brent and I call them communication killers and keepers. In the following pages, I explain each killer and it's opposing keeper.

Unspoken Expectations vs. No Givens

If you want to learn each other's language, you have to *speak*. So much of miscommunication is unspoken. We develop assumptions based on our own personal views and values. We have assumptions about how relationships operate, how they should be, and then these assumptions turn into expectations. But when those expectations are not talked about, there's trouble.

I was brought up in a home that taught if you weren't fifteen minutes early, you were late. Brent was brought up in a home where perpetual lateness was the norm. This became a huge issue for us, especially because of the nature of his crisis-driven career. I was offended and frustrated time after time because we could never get anywhere when I wanted to be there. After many discussions and tearful arguments, we learned to talk about the expectations each other had about time management.

Newlyweds Mark and Rachel had guests over for the evening. The weekend before, Rachel spent extra time cleaning the house, and she planted flowers in the backyard. Then she took off work early and prepared an appetizer to go with the drinks, made up the meal ahead of time, and put together a beautiful dessert. While the guests were there, Mark offered up some drinks and talked with the guys while he grilled the meat. All had a great evening with lots of laughs. Once the guests had gone, Mark declared he was exhausted and that he had to get up early for the day shift. He promptly went to bed. Rachel, who also had work the next morning, stayed up late cleaning up after everyone, fuming. She didn't talk to Mark for two days.

Before you get too angry with Mark, you must understand something. His mother was a stay-at-home mom who did *everything* for her family. She cooked dinner every night and cleaned up afterward without batting an eye. He had absolutely no clue how much work goes into entertaining, much less thoughts about helping to clean up. His unspoken expectation was that Rachel would handle it. Rachel, on the other hand, neglected to voice her expectation that he help with clean up because she assumed he would. His ignorance and her anger were both a result of unspoken expectations that neither of them were aware of.

Expectations do not kill communication; failing to express them does.

Mark and Rachel would have had a much different outcome had they taken a few minutes to discuss each other's responsibilities beforehand. It wouldn't have been much for him to clear the table and load the dishwasher while she rinsed. The whole evening was a success until Rachel was offended by her own assumptions.

Take the time to understand expectations for events, your job, even day-to-day things. Then negotiate solutions to those expectations. There are no givens!

Unforgiveness vs. Keeping Short Account

When our unspoken expectations are not met, it is very easy to develop resentment. We take it personally. It's an affront! But that really isn't fair, is it? How can our husbands know they did something wrong if they don't know the rules?

Years ago when Brent was working swing shift, he'd normally get off around midnight. One night in particular, he called me from the office to say that he had to write some reports and wouldn't be home for awhile. About two thirty a.m., I woke up and discovered he wasn't there yet. So I called the office. They told me he'd left about a half hour earlier. Because I assumed he'd be there any minute, I waited up for him. In the meantime Brent stopped to fuel up on the way home and struck up a conversation with the gas attendant. They had a very deep, meaningful conversation that lasted about two hours. By the time Brent drove up, I was convinced he was dead and then decided he was having an affair. Either way he would need a funeral! And, of course, I'd planned it all out.

After I unleashed my full fury on him, he told me what happened. He apologized, and I forgave him. Now we laugh about the string of obscenities that flowed from my mouth when I rarely cuss. And that is that.

Unforgiveness will not only kill communication, it will kill your relationship and could eventually kill your soul. No matter how you look at it, you lose. The thing that will keep communication flowing is keeping a short account. Let the anger go.

Victoria M. Newman

Brent calls this the emotional bank account. When we spend time together, do favors for each other, have good sex, etc., we are making deposits into the relationship. Arguments, harsh words, unspoken or demanding expectations, slamming doors, etc., are withdrawals from your relationship. Just like money, you look at your account at the end of each month, and hopefully your account is in the black. But too many withdrawals will cause it to fall into the red.

The currency of your relationship isn't cash; it's trust. When there isn't enough give for the take, you run into problems. When Brent was unaccounted for late into the night, fear consumed me. It was a big withdrawal. But when we decided he would phone home if a situation like this came up again (and it did), we made a deposit into our account. When I decided to let it go by forgiving him, we were in the black again. He learned from it too and never made that type of mistake again.

Unkindness vs. Setting Speech Boundaries

As a law enforcement family, there will always be pressures as we looked at in the first chapter. Unfortunately the easiest place to release that pressure is on those closest to us. And the closer you get, the worse it can be. Because we are so entwined, when our spouses go through stuff, it affects us and vice versa.

Earlier I mentioned a brush that went flying through the air at Brent on Christmas morning. The pressures at that moment were very great; we were newlyweds, we just moved, we didn't know anyone, we didn't have any money, and he was dealing with people on the road for the first time—it was nuts. That pressure really built up in me, and then when we fought Christmas morning, look out! She's gonna blow! And blow I did.

But it doesn't always go that way. What about when we're irritated with each other, or the kids, or the neighbor's dog that kept us up all night? Unkindness has a way of creeping in. We start treating each other poorly. Little digs here and there, our voices raise a bit, our patience wears thin. It gets old quick.

After our argument on Christmas morning, Brent and I settled down enough to decide that we needed to implement some ground rules. Here's what we came up with:

The first thing we decided was to never use divorce as a threat. We have friends who do, but we decided that this was too big of a withdrawal for us both. Brent's parents divorced when he was young, so divorce is painful for him. I came into our relationship with trust issues caused by philandering ex-boyfriends. We chose to treat this topic as taboo. The commitment that we made has helped us to do this. We *never* go there.

Second, we don't use sarcasm. When there are unresolved conflicts in a relationship, sarcasm is easy to muster. But it is also a cowardly way to throw insults. Someone says something mean and then laughs it off as a joke. It's not a joke. It hurts just as much. And

Victoria M. Newman

usually sarcasm is used when other people are around. Let me just say if you use sarcasm against your spouse in front of other people, you just created an embarrassing situation and cast a shadow on your own character. They'll think you're a jerk whether you are or not.

The third boundary we set is that we will never insult each other. This includes name calling, comparing with other people, and just being mean.

This doesn't mean that we don't joke or tease. But jokes and teasing are not meant to cut someone down but rather to lighten up. In fact humor is an excellent way to release some pressure.

One last thing. Something that comes really easy to us women is nagging. Many times our guys don't get things done in a timely manner whether it's because they tend to procrastinate or their schedules just don't allow for it. Either way, nagging is destructive. It won't get us what we're hoping for, which is action. Because my husband's job is so high velocity, he needs down time on the weekends and time with our kids. Weeks will go by with his honey-do list untouched. I am so tempted to nag, nag, and nag some more!

But over the years I have learned to combat this urge with these two ideas:

1. I'll ask supportive questions like "I know you've been working so hard lately. Is there anything I can do to help you get this done?" Many times there is a reason he can't get it done. Perhaps he has to research how to do

it, or the hardware store didn't have the right part. Many times I might be able to help him get past the obstacle, and then it gets done.

2. I tattle on him to my journal. It may seem a little silly, but it works. When I get to the point where I want to nag (or release frustration in other ways), I write it out and then throw it away. Actually, when I do this, it helps me work through the emotion so I can see the deeper issue. Then I'm in a much better position to communicate constructively.

Selfishness vs. Listen with the Desire To Understand

This last communication killer is so common it's actually part of our culture. We're encouraged to look out for ourselves, to be self-focused. We're also naturally inclined to respond to our own desires, feelings, and whims. We've been doing it since we could breathe. Maturity comes when you can keep your selfish tendencies in check, thinking and acting as if others are important too.

In a way your husband has sworn to the department that he will set selfishness aside, that he would lay down his life to save another. This is unselfishness at its best, real hero quality. You, as his wife, have agreed to share him for the greater good, another unselfish quality.

But in the day to day, we each have needs and wants that call to be met. We have dreams to pursue and goals to accomplish. So it's a dichotomy, making sure

Victoria M. Newman

that we take care of ourselves but also tending to the needs of our husbands, kids, work, etc.

If we really want an outstanding relationship, we will make a choice to listen with a desire to understand each other. But it requires character—humility, even— to set yourself aside for a time to listen.

Roger Williams, Director of the Mount Hermon Conference Center once said, "Selfish people will never live in unity." In marriage, everything needs to be filtered through *us*. Not "me," but "we." And the "we" includes you both—sometimes him, sometimes you, and sometimes both. There's a give and take here. And it takes practice.

Power Trip

This is a difficult chapter. Good communication requires responses that don't always come naturally. It takes courage and inner strength to speak the truth in a way that doesn't leave our partners wounded. But understand something, ladies: you have power. You have the power to crush your husband, to let your frustration fly in his face, or slowly, methodically undermine him. Either way, it could reduce him to shreds. The closer you grow, the more dangerous you become. You and I both know some women who are very good at this.

But you also have an opportunity to use your power to do something incredible. You have a choice to build him up into the man he deserves to be. Your love and respect can build strength and confidence in him. You can strengthen that thin blue line, indirectly, through careful, proactive words and actions—words that encourage, even heal; actions that respect who he is.

Discussion Group Questions

1. What is your love language? What is your husband's? How can you tell?

2. Name one unspoken expectation that has come up in your marriage.

3. What is one communication killer you deal with at home?

Chapter 5:
Game Face: Understanding Your Man

Two extremes exist every day in the life of a police officer. The problem is, if the officer and family are not aware of the hypervigilance cycle and its potential destruction, they can't be expected to take the appropriate corrective action and avoid the devastating effects on both their personal and professional lives.

Dr. Kevin Gilmartin[5], former cop and behavioral scientist

Michelle sat on the bed, watching Greg dress. She chattered away, recounting a conversation from dinner with girlfriends the night before. Irritated, Greg looked at her with that cop-look in his eye and scolded, "Not the time." He shoved his gun in the holster and walked out.

How many times have we witnessed a form of this scenario? They're getting ready for work, and we're enjoying their last few minutes at home. But somehow we innocently manage to irritate them. It took years for me to understand that when my husband puts on his uniform and weaponry, he has to put on his mind armor as well.

What he does requires body and mind, even a little of his soul. It's a war mentality to steel his mind to deal with whatever will come his way that shift. Even harmless chit-chat can be irritating as he's putting on his game face. He must be on his game mentally.

Understanding His Mentality

To be a cop is to be many different occupations all at once. He has to be an athlete, a soldier, a scientist, a researcher, a paramedic, a NASCAR driver, a gun expert and marksman, a counselor, a chemist, a diplomat, a wrestler, a runner, a mechanic, a writer, and a lawyer. He must have a mother's intuition, the nose of a bloodhound, the patience of a farmer, the compassion of Mother Teresa, and the tenacity of a 2-year-old. He must make peace out of chaos, comfort the anguished, discern criminal behavior from stupidity, and make split second decisions that may have life-altering consequences. He's expected to be polite when verbally abused, keep people safe in dangerous situations, respect those who disrespect him, and understand the intentions of those who are misbehaving. He must constantly confront evil, and remain unsullied. He must be quick to respond, though sometimes the calls stack up. He must be able to speak police shorthand on radios that may be difficult to hear, especially when

Victoria M. Newman

in heavy or fast-moving traffic. He is constantly second guessed on his actions, criticized for his demeanor, mocked for his diet and feared for his authority. He's a threat, a target, a punisher, yet is a rescuer, a protector, and in some cases, a savior.

Given these considerations, society's expectations on our law enforcement are just short of impossible. But day to day, they report for duty, not knowing what the shift will offer. They put on their badges and try to do the best they can to fulfill the expectations of those they serve. With these pressures in mind, it's our privilege to be not-so-silent partners behind the badge. Our influence backs them up where they tank up, gear up, and man up to be who they need to be and to do what they're expected to do.

Understanding His Motivation

"War is seductive. There's something inside me that lures me to the mission. I look at what's goin' down and know that I have to do what it takes to rescue these men… It's almost like I have this need, deep inside of me…" The soldier's eyes were moist and serious like he was reliving his combat experience again. I could see the pain on his face as images flashed through his mind's eye.

"And then, as I heard the bullets whiz by my head, I came to my senses. What am I doing? I have kids… I have a job at home… why am I taking these risks?"

It was a crowded room, but I didn't notice anything else. It was the closest thing I'd heard yet that describes the warrior mentality. Although I couldn't step into his shoes, it resonated within me. Duty. Compassion. Laying down one life for another. Courage that comes from deep within. I'd seen glimpses of this before in my husband and his co-workers. This is the mind of a man in uniform.

Some are born with it. Some learn it really young when they're watching Daddy put on his badge. Some are enticed by the honor and respect that goes with the shield and gun. No matter where they got it, it's there. It's a powerful, inner force that drives them on.

Only 3 percent of the general population can do what our husbands do.[6] They are willing to complete what's necessary in each situation. They may even lay down their lives to stop a criminal from producing chaos and death, and that willingness commands respect. Do you respect your husband for who he is? For what he values?

My friend Deidra has had a difficult time with this in her twenty-year marriage. He may be a hero out on the road, but it wasn't always the case at home. She and I had a conversation recently and this is what she said:

> In their line of work, they get respect. When people see a cop, they definitely clean up their act a little. Then he comes home, and I don't give him that respect. Why don't I give him that respect? Because some of the things he says are

Victoria M. Newman

not respectful! When you're acting like a jerk, why should I respect you?

One of my biggest failures has been that I haven't valued him. I haven't valued his accomplishments, the fact that he is putting his life on the line for other people, that he's a great provider, a great husband, and a great father. When I don't respect him, he feels really bad about himself. And that affects a lot of things, like our relationship. He feels like a failure because he thinks I don't believe in him. They get this level of respect on the road, and then when they get home, we don't give it. I think it's degrading. I wish I could go back and do it over again… to be more proud of him. I *am* proud of him.

Diedra and her cop have been married a long time and have a good marriage. But she is realizing now that the way she treats him affects him as a man and as a police officer. Respect is to a man what love is to a woman. It's their greatest need. We as wives can remember that there is always something to value within our husbands even when they're not faring well in other areas. It helps to remember him as a whole rather than honing in on his weaknesses.

Understanding His Moods

In his book *Emotional Survival for Law Enforcement Officers,* Dr. Kevin Gilmartin describes the highs and lows of what he calls the hypervigilance rollercoaster. To be vigilant is to stay watchful and alert to danger or trouble. But because our men never know what will come at them on any given call, they maintain a state of hypervigilance throughout their shift. They are programmed for survival to overcome whatever they deal with while on duty, and that requires much more than just a pep talk to themselves as they go out the door.

Their bodies and minds sustain this level of hypervigilance throughout the shift. But what goes up must come down, even physiologically. After his shift is over, he retreats home to you and your family, but his mind and body are exhausted from maintaining a high level of watchful intensity. Rather than returning to a normal level, his mind and body go to a place below normal to recuperate. The next day it's repeated. And the next. Eventually, this wears him (and you!) down. If you ignore this rollercoaster, it can lead to a breakdown in his emotional health, which will have a huge impact on you and your marriage.

If you have an understanding of what is going on inside his body and mind, the good news is you are a big component of helping him through it. Dr. Gilmartin says,

> ...[T]he rollercoaster sets up officers to think, act, and live like victims, to not invest their energy, emotions, and sense of self in the phase of the rollercoaster that they do in fact control, the bottom or off-duty phase. It's a clear

Victoria M. Newman

catch-22: Officers must maintain hypervigilance to perform and survive on the streets and practice good officer safety, yet it is this same hypervigilance that can cause officers to relinquish control of their personal lives. They cannot lower the upper phase of the rollercoaster. They must maintain the elevated physical state of heightened awareness of potential risk while functioning as officers. Without training and awareness of the rollercoaster, officers return home and experience the pendulum effect... *Ironically, it is the nonpolice support systems that, when they remain intact, determine if the officers remain good cops for the duration of the entire police career...* (emphasis mine)[7]

You are the first and foremost non-police support system. Understanding this process gives you a chance to deal with it. You can help him maintain balance by creating balance. Things like exercise, vacations, hobbies, and activities will pull him out of that below normal level his body wants to retreat to. Take time to rejuvenate as a couple and as a family during his off-duty time, keeping this phenomenon in mind.

Before and After Shifts

Many times this hypervigilance rollercoaster will begin just before he leaves for work. He's putting on his game face. For Brent and I, the time before his shift wasn't pretty for years. Sometimes I'd be upset half the shift after he'd leave. He was intensely focused. There were a few hurt feelings here and there. I finally learned he needed his space to gear up for the day. It wasn't directed at me. He was inwardly focused to be on his game.

I also needed to be careful about the demands I placed on him right before work. A half hour before he was to leave was not a good time to talk about bills or problems with the kids or scheduling conflicts. I learned to make a list for later. A little patience and everyone benefits.

For many officers, coming home is a lot of the same. In addition to that coming down from hypervigilance, a bad accident, a supervisor's comment, or an incident involving children will sometimes bother your officer, and he needs down time to think it through. Your questions or requests may conflict with his thinking time and his comfort in bringing up something so raw. You never know what he's dealt with that day. How do we handle their responses like strong, mature women?

Faye has implemented the pause moment. She'll ask her husband how his day was and pause for the signs she's come to recognize after thirteen years on the force. Sometimes he'll be fine. Other times she'll hear a heavy sigh, and so she'll remain silent. She knows that if he needs to call one of two fellow officers that something is bugging him and that he'll let her know in his time. She then adjusts to his response as appropriate.

Communication comes first—verbal and non-verbal. If he's bothered about something, maybe he needs a trip to the gym. Maybe he just needs to hold his baby daughter for a while in silence or wrestle loudly with his boys. Maybe he needs to watch TV for a couple of hours and relax. The rub comes when you have plans for the evening. Or it's tag-team time and it's your turn to go to work. This happens over and over through the year and beyond. It's learning to ebb and flow with the moment and having the awareness and self-control to deal with this process positively.

I want him to be on his game when he needs to be and, if he isn't to let me know so I can deal with it and move on. But nine times out of ten, it's difficult to do. He doesn't know what's on his mind; he's just irritable. Or he doesn't have the energy to articulate his needs. Sometimes he just lies on the bed and falls asleep. So much for dinner!

Brent has learned to be good about telling me when he is so spent he can't meet my expectations (at least the majority of the time). I have had to learn to be patient, and that right there is tough. Sometimes it just stinks! And I've decided that it's okay. When we understand that it isn't us, fight the temptation to panic or worry, and communicate like mature people, that's when it gets better. We develop thick skin. But it's keeping our hearts soft and bitterness-free over time that takes a bit more energy and focus.

I've been talking a lot about flexibility and allowing your man to decompress from his job. But by no means am I suggesting you take a doormat mentality. You are an equal part of your marriage and have equal value. As cop wives, we tend to be strong and sometimes outspoken, but not all of us. I'm suggesting ways to come alongside and support, but in the context of mutual love and respect for one another. There is a difference between being interdependent (the goal) and co-dependent.

In the long term, we need to find ways to achieve balance. When Brent took over command of the CHP Academy, we were mentally prepared that it would take a lot of out of us. He worked long hours and maneuvered a large staff through some seemingly impossible demands. At times it was downright overwhelming. During these times he'd come home, share a bit with me, and we'd sit together, shaking our heads.

I wish I could share that we took advantage of his vacation time and gave him the down time he needed. But that wasn't the case. He actually built so much time up that he exceeded his vacation time limits. And we suffered as a couple and as a family. It has been the hardest season to go through in his career.

After two years of long days and many weekends, he wanted to umpire baseball games. I reluctantly agreed. It seemed at first like it was just more time away from our family. But when I saw the camaraderie he built with other guys and how happy he was when he returned, I didn't mind that he was gone the extra hours. I finally saw him relax. It became a replenishment, something he desperately needed.

During this time at the academy, my life was busy as well. He was busy with his job, and I was busy with my own pursuits. But one thing I did during this time was be available to listen when he came home. For much of our marriage, my guy didn't talk much about work. He usually had a lengthy commute to calm down. But as the academy commander, he entered the house, still talking on his phone. Because he couldn't talk with others about his frustrations, he vented to me. I was safe, I listened. I didn't say much, didn't need to. Sometimes I offered my female intuition, and he was pleasantly surprised that I could be so business smart. I liked that. It brought a new level of trust and respect to our relationship. All I had to do was be ready to close my mouth and open my ears.

The Hero at Home

Because this book covers different aspects of law enforcement marriage, it probably seems like my entire existence revolves around the fact that he is a cop. It doesn't. There are areas of our lives that have nothing whatsoever to do with law enforcement. This is a big question for new officers' wives. "I have my own job; do I have to drop everything for this to work?" The answer is no. Life is life. Kids. Careers. Hobbies. Church. Clubs. Sports. There is more to life than law enforcement.

Erica doesn't view her husband as a hero when he walks in the door. He's Marlo, the father of her children, the man she married, and the one who takes out the trash. So when he comes home, she expects him to jump into their lives. I love this. Erica has two boys and a job. She basically runs the home and likens it to a revolving machine. When Marlo comes home from his shift, she expects him to join their lives that are already in motion. Because she has communicated this, it works!

What you don't know about Erica is she had to face that horrible moment that we all fear: "Honey, I need you to come the hospital. I've just been shot!" Marlo called her from his stretcher on the side of the freeway. After this critical incident, she had to make things click in her mind. This was when she adopted this attitude: Marlo is the man she married. He's not Marlo the hero; he's Marlo the husband. He's Marlo the dad. In fact, she's only seen Officer Marlo a few times.

This mindset may be more difficult for other men. When they are on duty, they have to take control in the midst of chaos. Your man has been trained to be in control of situations and will be direct and to the point. He doesn't do multiple choice on duty. What happens when he comes home, still in this attitude of control?

My guess is it doesn't go over well. I know this might be pretty tempting for cops to do, but it doesn't exactly pan out at home. We've been running things all day, and it's a little difficult to relinquish that position. We've got our tried and true ways of making it work, and then he comes in and does it differently! Again, this is where respectful communication comes in. He

Victoria M. Newman

needs to be a part of the home too, so don't hold on so tightly to your methods. On the other hand, you are not one of his customers, and he doesn't want you to be.

The other side of the spectrum is that they are tired of making decisions and/or babysitting crooks all day, and they don't want to take the reins at home at all. Recall the down stage of the hypervigilance roller coaster. It takes some good talks and patience to work through this.

The Long-term Perspective

I've mentioned several things that you see on a day to day basis—the short term. But there is a long-term perspective as well. In a career that spans twenty to thirty years, these issues will ebb and flow with the seasons. Supervisors and commanders come and go, and, depending on their leadership skills or lack thereof, your husband's career will benefit or suffer.

There have been seasons that Brent couldn't wait to get to work. And there were times when his stress was so elevated his blood pressure would reflect it. The point here is that seasons come and go. Enjoy the good times and embrace the rough spots for the character building they can instill. Either way, sometimes it just helps to know that it won't be forever.

His Coping Mechanisms

Your cop will have his ways to deal with stress. You may not be crazy about some of them, but, if it's working, you need to let it go. A couple of years ago, Brent had a chief who dealt with stress by having an occasional outdoor cigar-smoking session with a few guys in the office. My daughters hated this. They always knew when Daddy smoked a cigar that day. But I knew that a few cigars over a several month period were unlikely to do any damage. In fact, it did him some good to take an occasional timeout in the middle of a hard work day.

Debriefing with their friends seems to help them deal with stuff a bit easier. Suggest he play racquetball or golf with some buddies. Maybe a yearly hunting trip is in order, or have him spend a morning fishing with a friend. During these times, it'll also help your attitude if you schedule something for yourself.

Cop humor, silence, Monday-night football, motorcycle riding, exercise… our guys need outlets. There has to be some way for them to fill up. He's putting out a lot of himself to be an officer. You can help too by listening, taking care of your portion of the marriage partnership, initiating sex, and creating a safe home. But as awesome as you are, you are not the only place he can be filled. Support an outlet or two that build him up.

Our Response

Understanding our men—who they are, what they do, how they deal with it—helps us to know better how to support them. But this is only half of it. How we respond is the other half.

Erica, whom I referred to earlier in this chapter, says that she doesn't think about this stuff each and every day he walks out the door. I don't either. But I suggest thinking through it ahead of time when all is well, letting these thoughts digest so that day to day and year to year we grow and learn together instead of moving apart. In some ways, it's putting on our own mind armor to keep us in the marriage game as well.

We have a choice here. We can begrudge the way they are and build a wall to protect our sense of who we think they should be. We could, over time, harden our hearts toward parts of them and complain behind their backs to our friends. We could demand that they change, and they might even try out of love for us. But, in the end, they will not be able to trust us completely.

Or we can accept them for who and what they are, respecting their processes. We can love them unconditionally for what they are and be forgiving for what they aren't. This acceptance gives them the freedom to be real. And in the security that this provides, they might even just mellow out over time. I've witnessed this in many marriages. We might say, "She's been good for him." At the very least they will appreciate the safe place that our love creates and trust us with depths of themselves we will treasure. Sex may be better, too, as the walls of mistrust disappear and we grow in intimacy.

On its surface, it seems like an easy choice. But it isn't. Marriage is hard. Marriage to a cop is even harder. How can we get the courage necessary to thrive amidst all of this?

Discussion Group Questions

1. How does your husband wind down/relax from his work day? Do you feel this is working for him, you, and your kids?

2. Do you recognize symptoms of the hyper-vigilance rollercoaster in your husband? Elaborate.

3. What is an attitude that you feel you need to tweak that will improve your relationship with your husband?

Chapter 6:
Thick Skin, Soft Heart: How To Deal Emotionally

I don't wear the badge on a uniform. But when you're married to an officer, you wear the shadow of their badge on your heart.

> Pat, wife of a CHP officer
> who was injured on-duty

Worrying is carrying tomorrow's load with today's strength—carrying two days at once. It is moving into tomorrow ahead of time. Worry does not empty tomorrow of its sorrow, it empties today of its strength.

> Corrie Ten Boom, Holocaust survivor

In 2006, one of our officers responded to an accident that involved a disturbed young man. One thing led to another, and a fight ensued as the man tried to steal the officer's gun. A sheriff's deputy joined in, as did a paramedic who was on the scene. The subject was overpowered, and he went to jail. This kind of thing happens often, but this time a reporter with a camera just happened to stop and snap several pictures of the entire incident. The photos made their way to a variety of places, and *Code 3 Magazine* picked them up and published them.

In response, they received an emotional letter from a wife of a police officer with three small children. She wrote that she was shocked to see such graphic pictures and didn't wish to receive the magazine anymore. In the next issue, there were several responses to her letter. Here are two excerpts:

> ...[B]elieve in your husband... and support him with all your heart. It is for you, your children and the world they live in that he serves as a peace officer. You are and need to be a part of that. A loved one's support and faith is often the secret weapon that a peace officer will use to survive a critical incident. Hiding from reality will not work.
>
> Deputy sheriff married to
a highway patrolman

> Being an officer's spouse is not for the faint of heart. It takes strength, will and an understanding for the love of the job that officers feel and commit themselves to... I hope she can come to terms with that which she is now married to. If not, her constant fear will destroy both her and her marriage...
>
> Former officer and wife of police officer[8]

Fear had taken its toll on this young mother, and it seemed that she responded with avoidance and anger. It's a natural instinct but one that could be destructive to her and her family. So, what's a girl to do?

Life, Liberty, and the Pursuit of Happiness

Worry and fear are chronic when the ground you stand on isn't firm enough to steady you. Every house is built upon a foundation, and the house will only be as sound as the materials it's built upon. If your personal foundation is built upon things like truth, morality, goodness, and a love for others, chances are you're standing on something solid that will withstand the storms life brings you. But if you are standing on ignorance, selfishness, fear of what could happen at any moment, or are led primarily by your senses (touch, sight, taste, etc.), your life will eventually falter on these shifting sands.

What is it that you stand on as an individual? What are your goals for your life? What drives you? When you are eighty years old, what do you want your life to look like as you take inventory of the years you invested? The answers to these questions will determine your success in life as a person, a wife, a mother and levels of satisfaction or regret at the end of your life. It will also determine your emotional stability in the face of what your husband's career hands you.

Most women that I talk to want to be happy. That's what life is all about, right? We don't want trouble, we don't want pain. We want to feel good inside and out, have fun, live positive lives with positive thinking. It's life, liberty, and the pursuit of happiness.

Unfortunately, if we are actively pursuing happiness, we are headed for disappointment, maybe even sorrow. Let me tell you why. Happiness is subjective. Happiness is elusive. And the definition of happiness is ever changing, depending on what it is that we chase to fill that happy place.

My youngest son recently wanted a Wii so bad he could taste it. He researched it on the web. He saved his money for months. Whenever we went shopping, he asked to swing by the electronics section just to see if they had them in stock. His pursuit of happiness was wrapped up in buying that Wii. Finally the day came when he received his Wii in the mail. For the next few weeks, he played Wii for hours. And, yes, he was so happy! But after a couple months, I noticed he was researching something else on the computer—catcher's gear. Here we go again!

Happiness is short lived. There will be times in your marriage that you will not be happy. There will be seasons that will take you down some dark paths. If your underlying pursuit is to be happy, you may want out in these seasons. Why? Because chasing a feeling that comes and goes will be a constant source of disappointment. And in that emotional instability, you will inadvertently undermine your own marriage.

Victoria M. Newman

Short-Term vs. Long-Term Thinking

Pursuing happiness is short-term thinking. It concentrates on right now. Right now I'd be very happy if I had a big piece of German chocolate cake. And then after I eat that very large piece of German chocolate cake, I'd be happy if I had just a little more. So I'll eat another half piece. Fifteen minutes later, I'll be miserable because my stomach hurts. And then in the morning when my jeans are too tight, the guilt sets in. Long-term thinking is different. This mindset understands that passing on that dessert means better-fitting jeans, and that is the avenue to self-respect and good health. It is making a decision to pass on something that will make me happy temporarily to obtain something much more satisfying in the long run. Long-term thinking is realizing that when I am happy, I celebrate it because there will be seasons that I will not be happy. And yet I'm okay with it.

Long-term thinking in our marriages requires looking at the goal: to still have a thriving marriage at the end of our lives. Actively pursuing a satisfying, contented marriage means investing in your relationship over the years in happy and not-so-happy times.

Long-term thinking doesn't blow things out of proportion when you have a spat this week after connecting on a deep level last week. Relationships ebb and flow, and short-term thinking will create drama. "You never…" is the accusation when, in actuality, he does at times just not enough for you or not enough at the moment. Drama gets tiresome when it pops up again and again. It takes out large withdrawals from your marital bank account. In contrast, long-term thinking relaxes a bit and doesn't panic. Long-term thinking stops taking cues from whatever doesn't feel right at the moment and tries to understand the big picture.

Put Fear in Its Place

The most common thing cops' wives hear from non-cops are questions about how we deal with fear. It's the first thing thought about once a loved one decides law enforcement is the career they want to do, and it's the most obvious. Those on the outside looking in assume that we worry all the time and the circumstances dictate to what degree. When Brent promoted to lieutenant and was relegated to a desk, our non-cop friends figured that I wouldn't worry as much because he was out of the danger zone. They were surprised to hear that I didn't worry as a lifestyle; that I had dealt with my fear long ago.

The first time I felt fear about my husband's job was about nine months in. He came home one morning and told me how he and his partner came upon a gang fight in a bad part of Los Angeles. Being the eager rookies they were, they stopped, called for back up, pulled their guns, and yelled freeze. And those who were fighting did freeze, unbelievably enough. All except for one, who took off running. At that point Brent's partner gave chase, leaving Brent alone with twenty armed gang members, having only a six-bullet revolver and a shotgun. It was at that point he realized that the situation could go really bad. He was outnumbered in people and in weapons. They could've turned on him in a heartbeat...but they didn't.

It seemed like forever, but soon he heard the cavalry coming; others arrived, black and whites screeching in from all directions. Gang members were sorted out, handcuffed, and taken to jail. Brent's partner came back too with the fleeing suspect in custody. Turns out one of the bad guys was wanted for rape. It all turned out well, but the fear factor was definitely there.

Brent laughed about it—and at first, so did I. But it scared me. I started counting down the "what ifs," and fear crept in with them. Honey, we're not in Chico anymore! He's fighting real gangs with real guns. The danger was near, and it was very *real*.

At some point in your husband's career, you will face fear. Some of the wives I've talked to said the first year was the hardest, and then they settled down. Some of you have a natural tendency to worry, and this is hard for you. There are still others who hardly worry at all until they come face to face with a reminder that what their husbands do *is* dangerous.

Rosa told me that she was having trouble with fear. Her husband had graduated from the academy just three months earlier and then was sent to Oakland. I understood; in the last month there were two separate shooting incidents with our department alone and a riot deployment. A year earlier Oakland Police

Department lost four officers to a single shooter. It was a dangerous place. She wondered how to deal with it.

When fear rears its ugly head, how can we deal with it? I think the answer lies in what we choose to put our trust in. What is it that we can hold on to that will be adequate to stand up to the "what ifs?" Let's look at a few facts—they're in our favor.

According to the National Employment Matrix, there were more than 1.2 million law enforcement members in the United States in 2008. During 2009, there were 116 deaths of American law enforcement officers, according to LawOfficer.com. Concerns of Police Survivors estimates on their website that 140 to 160 American officers lose their lives on duty every year. This is still too many on-duty deaths, but you can clearly see the odds here. Police officers are not even listed as one of the ten most deadly jobs.[9]

There is a great deal of time, energy, thought, and money that goes into the training that your husband receives and continues to receive throughout his career. There are many people throughout the country whose jobs are to reduce the amount of injuries and deaths of police officers. Law enforcement training is designed to provide each officer the mindset and tactics to make it home at the end of each shift.

The same can be said about protective gear. There are constant revisions and improvements in body armor, tools, and weaponry. My husband receives several catalogs a year to unveil the latest technologies available to law enforcement.

But we still lose excellent officers every year. It is a possibility no matter what the odds. So, how can we protect ourselves?

If something should go awry and you experience an injury or death, information is power; educate yourself. Here are several proactive steps you can take to ensure you are protected in these situations.

1. Do research on what your department provides for the families of fallen officers. In many cases, there may not be monetary benefits, but they might support you through assistance programs and help with funerals.

2. Look at federal and state benefits available to you.

3. Make sure your husband's life insurance and accidental death/dismemberment is adequate for the needs of your family.

4. Draw up a will and provide a copy to the executer.

5. Keep your beneficiary information updated.

6. Ensure that your spouse keeps your contact information updated in the records at work (i.e., new address, phone numbers).

7. Have a conversation with your spouse about final wishes, how he wants to be buried and where, details he may want at his funeral,

etc. If you can't do this, have him write it down and keep in a safe place.

8. Know that police survivors have a strong support community through Concerns of Police Survivors (COPS). Their website has a wealth of information, and should you have to face this, there are local chapters you can contact.

Proactive Steps To Deal with Fear

We can know the odds and be prepared for the worst. But there are always those close calls and creepy little feelings that come up from time to time. How do we disarm them?

1. Face the worst case scenario. Much of what we fear is unknown, and fear breeds worry. Think through your greatest fear and play it out in your mind as to how you will deal with it. Come up with an emergency response to the "what if."

2. Demystify the experience. Familiarize yourself with your agency's death benefits and protocol. Talk to your spouse about who you would want to deliver the news should something happen. Security is very important to us as women, and not knowing what will happen *if* can be a catalyst for worry. Brent's

agency encourages officers to designate who will notify next of kin in case. You can be a part of that decision or work to initiate such a protocol in your husband's agency.

3. Resist the temptation to listen to scanners or dispatch applications on the Internet. This is not an emergency response to facing the worst case scenario. This is a distracting illusion of control. "If I just know what's going on, I can handle it…" Risky approach. This could perpetuate fear, not dispel it.

4. Talk out your fears. I talked with Brent in his down time once or twice and found it helpful. I've also talked with other seasoned wives, and this helps too. You may even consider talking with a survivor if you have the opportunity. If you are a person of faith, prayer is an excellent way to talk out your fears. Personally, this is where I found much comfort when I have dealt with occasional fear.

5. Let it go. This is one area you can't control, and if you try you'll drive yourself and others crazy. Go back to your foundation. What or who is it that you trust?

My friend Michelle Walker lost her husband in the line of duty New Year's Eve of 2005. I asked her how she dealt with fear before he was killed. I learned that her father was with LAPD and had suffered a shooting but recovered. Incredibly, she never feared that her husband would be killed. She answered, "Fear drains your energy, puts stress on your marriage and family, and ultimately won't change a thing. I'm so glad that I didn't waste the time I had with Mike worrying."

When I Moved In, I Brought My Baggage

Jim and Angie sat across from us, their meals barely touched. They recounted an issue that they couldn't get past in their marriage, and it was huge. They were so concerned that they brought it to Brent and I, their mentors, to help them sort it out. About that time Brent asked, "Is this something that you struggled with in your home life growing up?" Jim's face froze, and I could almost see the light bulb brighten above his head. He then recalled a story that had paralleled their issue to the tee. The core issue was apparent to each one of us, and they came up with a simple way to deal with it.

In this life journey you've been on, chances are you have picked up things along the way that aren't so good. Someone hurt you. You have adopted others' destructive messages about yourself. Perhaps you made poor choices in your past, and you are reaping the consequences now. Whatever the reason for the hurts in your life, if not dealt with, they can adversely affect your marriage.

Dr. Gil Stieglitz, in his book entitled *Marital Intelligence – A Foolproof Guide to Saving and Strengthening*

Victoria M. Newman

Marriage, says that past baggage is one of five problems we face in marriage. He writes,

> We carry with us wounds and destructive internalized programming as well as guilt and consequences from our past actions. There is no way to seal off the past and have its unresolved issues stay away. At times the impact of unresolved past baggage is so strong that it must be dealt with before progress in marriage can be attempted... It will continue as is unless those wounds are exposed, grieved, and processed... People need to process their pain from the past.[10]

Many are the hurts of those we know. Some heal, some don't. Some make peace with their pain; others live in the past. If baggage is affecting your relationship, there are healthy ways to deal with it. Check your support system (see next chapter). Some things can be talked out with a wise friend. I also recommend going to an older, wiser couple with your husband. When Brent and I went through a tough time with one of our teenagers, we sought out the help of a couple we respected who'd gone through similar things with their son.

Counseling is also a great tool. I once heard a police officer say that when she needed help with plumbing she called a plumber. When she needed help with electrical, she called an electrician. So it only made sense when she needed help with some emotional issues she was facing, she called a counselor.

The Whole You

I've talked about motivation, foundations, problems, and trust. These are some deep parts of yourself you may never have thought about in this context. But I come back to them because it is so important to know who you are. When we know who we are, then we are much better equipped to deal with whatever life hands us. We know what will work and what won't. It's much better than going through life just guessing.

When Brent went into the academy to become a highway patrolman, I went through my own transformation at home (the CHP Academy is a six-month live-in arrangement with most weekends off). I had to stand on my own two feet for the first time in my life. I had a home to run, a job to perform, and on the weekends a husband to encourage and support. Back in the day before e-mail and cell phones, I had no way to get in touch with him during the week. I had to rely on his ability to use the one phone on campus while completing rigorous eighteen-hour days. He didn't call much, and I missed him terribly.

It was during this time that I discovered that my husband would not meet all of my needs. Fulfillment could not be found in him alone, nor could he secure my insecurities. This was hard to accept; I came into our marriage with an expectation that he would do all that. I did some soul-searching, found a mentor, and grew up a little. It was a good thing too because that toughened me up for our first assignment in Los Angeles.

The best approach to our relationship with our husbands is as whole people. They can meet some of our needs but not all. Spending some time answering the motivation and foundation questions is a good start. But we cannot do this alone. We must have a support system.

Discussion Group Questions

1. When you are eighty years old, what do you want your life to look like as you take inventory of the years you invested?

2. Do you struggle with fear and/or worry? If yes, what is something you're willing to try to combat it? If not, why not?

3. Do you tend to live with short-term thinking or long-term thinking?

Chapter 7:

Peeps and Props:
Your Support System

Two are better than one, because they have a
good return for their work;
If one falls down, his friend can help him up.
But pity the man who falls and has no one to
help him up!

Ancient proverb

It started with a funeral… All of our husbands
had to work it, so several of us went to Chili's,
ate chocolate cake, and cried together. We've
been close ever since.

Faye, CHP wife of 16 years

There was an instant connection with other
cops' wives. They could understand what I was
going through. It became a lifesaver.

Christina, wife of deputy sheriff

It was a mix and match evening. There were cops'
wives who were married from three to thirty-two

years. There were different departments, nationalities, ages, and viewpoints. We had a former dispatcher, a wife who had two sons on the force, and two wives of retired policemen. Several had gone through critical incidents and their aftermath with their husbands. Some had gone through struggles in their marriages and almost didn't make it. And yet the unity was undeniable. Those who'd never met before were hugging and exchanging numbers by the end of the night.

I hadn't expected this when I invited several wives of law enforcement to my home to talk about our lives. I was pleasantly surprised at their insight; heads nodded around the table as each took a turn to describe what being a wife of a law enforcement officer was like. At the end of the evening, several women said that even though they'd never done something like this, they wanted to do it again and soon.

I learned something that night. No matter our differences, we need each other.

A Need Indeed!

We have so many demands on our time. Work, children, and managing our homes consumes hours and energy. Add to that a husband's crisis-driven career, and there's not a lot of time for much else. We can live our lives moving from task to task, and there is a certain amount of satisfaction with this. But after awhile loneliness sets in. We need connection. We need to laugh together, cry together. We need someone to hear

Victoria M. Newman

the fifty thousand words we have to get out every day. And our kids just can't meet these needs.

The California Highway Patrol Academy holds two important events for every cadet class. The day before the cadets report for training, the staff hosts a family orientation seminar. The purpose is to educate loved ones as to what their cadet will go through and suggest ways to help them through the next twenty-seven weeks. The day before graduation, family members of those graduating are invited to a family support panel. The purpose of this meeting is to educate families for their first steps as an officer. In both events seasoned wives are invited to encourage, validate, and connect with other families. Swapping numbers with nearby people, encouraging Facebook connections and forums online, and grouping families according to geographical area of assignment is a big part of the connection process. The reason our department does this is that they have recognized the importance of support systems for our officers. It is becoming increasingly apparent that cops and their families need to have connection with and support from those who love them. Their emotional survival depends on it.

You and I are no different. We may be the support systems for our men in uniform, but we can't do it alone either. When we deal with what comes home, we need validation of our thoughts and actions. It is good to get feedback from those we trust, and most of all we need healthy doses of encouragement that come from others who love us. Living life together gives us confidence and security.

Let's start with you as an individual. Do you have close friends or family who support you, your marriage, and your kids? Chances are you have a great support system in place. But what if your husband's job takes you to another part of the state or country? Or you have a strained relationship with your mother? Or your spouse just started his career in law enforcement and your friends not only don't understand but also don't want to?

Brent and I have lived in several parts of our state as he's transferred for promotions. My experience is that I have been the one to take the initiative. In southern California, before I had children, my workplace was where I found my friends. I found myself tagging along with single girls when Brent was working or looked forward to ladies' nights out with coworkers. We went to the Hollywood Bowl together, threw wedding and baby showers, and went to lunch. I learned a lot about LA's creative variety hanging out with these gals.

Once I had children, it seemed to be a little easier to find friends. I joined a local Mothers of Preschoolers chapter and got involved. I was invited by another CHP wife and loved it. As the kids grew older, I met ladies at school functions and the gym. We'd work out and then go to coffee afterward for girl time.

One of my closest friends is a young woman who moved to Sacramento the same time I did, and we met in a Bible study. Once I learned her husband was with the Air Force and they lived five minutes away, our families began living our lives together almost every day. We have continued to keep in touch through the years and spend many of our vacations visiting them in whatever state they reside.

One question I hear often from new officers' wives is, "How do I get in touch with other law enforcement wives?" It's not as easy as it might seem. Sometimes you just have to extend an invitation for coffee without expectations. You never know who you'll connect with and who you won't. With the friend in the Air Force, I had to ask her several times to get together before she actually took me up on it. She and her husband weren't used to getting to know people much because they moved often. We cured them of that.

Annie's husband, Tim, was with county homicide. It was hard on him, and he wasn't the same person after he saw some awful things. I asked her how she dealt with it. She told me that in addition to her church, she has some great friends in law enforcement. She had grown close to a female deputy who was also married to an officer. When their husbands worked swing shift, they would take the kids out to have some fun. Sometimes they got home just before their husbands did! But Annie told me that those fun times were what got her and the kids through those long, lonely evenings.

Another thing that works fairly well within offices is to get groups of wives together on a regular basis, grass-roots style. The best example I've seen is what my friend Faye put together. She and a couple of ladies started going to coffee together. Then they went to a play. Soon they invited more and more ladies from the station to join them, and they came up with a variety of monthly events. Faye had the vision to connect the women in her husband's office, and she went for it. It caught on. Then when one of the women's husbands was killed in the line of duty, they stepped up and took care of her, comforting her and meeting practical needs. It was community they created, and it naturally kicked into action when crisis hit. Faye and I are now actively encouraging others to do the same thing in other areas of California.

Another way that we've seen great connection on a larger level is groups of law enforcement wives on the Internet. Our cadet wives have been creating small groups on Facebook. This is a great way to keep in touch with several people at once and when you don't live close to other wives. This is an incredible way to gain information, ask questions about benefits, support families through critical incidents and family emergencies, and just toss out ideas. When face to face isn't always available, this is a great way to connect. If you check my website, I have updated links to several groups of law enforcement wives on the Internet.

But Girls Are Mean!

I ran into an acquaintance recently who I hadn't seen in awhile. We quickly caught each other up on our families, and she mentioned that her nine-year-old daughter was giving her fits. I nodded, knowingly. "That's when their hormones start up," I shared. "I bet she's also experiencing drama with other girls at school, isn't she?" She looked at me like I was psychic. I went on to recall stories of my girls when they turned that magic number nine. It was a hurtful time; girls were so mean!

Sometimes interacting with other women is scary. We've all been there at some time or another—some girl is creating drama, and suddenly *connection* isn't such a hot idea. The good news is as we mature, there are fewer of us who take part in this kind of stuff. But definitely not all. That's why I say, "Proceed with caution!" If you find yourself connecting with a woman who is gossiping, run—don't walk—to the nearest exit. Even if she's talking trash about someone you don't like, chances are she'll eventually talk trash about you too.

Rules of Engagement

Over the years I have worked with, served, taught, mentored, spoke to, and counseled hundreds of women of all backgrounds. I've learned through trial and error how to be a friend and observed those that do friendship well. I've come up with some general rules of engagement that will help you pick some good friends and be a good friend in return.

The Number-One Golden Rule

I'll start with the most basic. We learned this in school or from our moms early on, but it represents a very good boundary for our behavior! The golden rule is to do to others what you would have them do to you. If you want someone to keep your secrets, keep hers. If kindness is important to you, then be kind. If you would like some practical help here and there, then offer and follow through with practical help. Fill in the blanks from there.

Keep this in mind as you converse with others. As women, we have a tendency to talk too much. Oh, the words we say, every day, in lots of ways! But we all have two ears and one mouth. Listening is twice as important as talking. Ooh, this is a good reminder for me! I have so many stories, and I like to tell those stories to make connections to this and that—show others how much we have in common! But I like to be listened to, so I have had to teach myself to shut my mouth and listen to others.

Rule Number Two: What's the Back Story?

Novelists are always on the lookout for creative ways to bring in the back story. This is the prelude to what you're reading in the book, the reasons or the road to how the character got where they are physically and emotionally in the story. The same goes for real people; there's *always* a back story.

I have learned to never make assumptions based on first impressions. Some women are shy. Some women want to be friends, but want to first observe if you're trustworthy or not. When I speak, it's often the women

Victoria M. Newman

who don't make eye contact with me during my talk that approach me afterwards to ask questions.

You'd be surprised how many women are carrying burdens that come across as indifference to others. Those who come across as confident, engaged women can actually be harboring feelings of self-doubt just beneath the surface.

Things aren't always as they appear. We don't always have the facts. That fabulously dressed brunette sitting by herself with a don't-approach-me look has a story. She probably isn't stuck up. She probably doesn't think she's better than you. She might be shy. Or she was abused as a child. Or she and her husband had an argument on the way there. Or she has ten dollars in her bank account and no groceries in the fridge. You never know what is behind the blank stare or the up front attitude. But it might be worth it to try to find out the back story. It just might be very similar to your own.

Rule Number Three: They Are One, Not Two

Rose's husband is a deputy with a nearby county sheriff's department. She was recounting to me how the office had experienced severe drama in the last several months, and it was wearing on her even though she wasn't directly involved. There were two people having an affair at the office—an officer who was married and the wife of another deputy. Everyone knew except the spouses, and they were all trying to keep it a secret while gossiping about it. What a mess.

You will socialize with other attractive men in uniforms throughout your husband's career. Chances are your friends' husbands are nice to look at too. But if we are to conduct ourselves in a way that makes us safe friends, we must establish boundaries with other men.

I have developed a defense mechanism against letting handsome men get into my thoughts. When I see a married man who is attractive, I make sure to meet his wife. Then I look at them as one entity, not two. When I see Robert, I see Sue. When I see Scott, I see Lisa. This has worked for me; it keeps my mind in check. Looking at them as a couple keeps me from flirting and therefore doesn't stir up bad vibes with my friends. The friendships keep me accountable. I don't even go there, and others sense that I'm trustworthy.

I also have to mention the way we dress. Women are beautiful. And how we clothe ourselves makes a big statement to others about who we are and what we value. Dressing to attract (very short skirts, low-cut tops, ultra tight pants) may get the attention of men, but it screams to other women that they can't trust her. She's unsafe, threatening. Dressing nicely but appropriately helps other women trust you as a friend.

Rule Number Four: Loose Lips Sink Ships!

Have you ever poured a bag of sugar into a canister and realized too late that it wasn't big enough to hold the whole bag? There are sugar crystals everywhere! They're on the counter, the floor, and your clothes. You

Victoria M. Newman

can sweep for the next three days and still feel them on your shoes.

This is what happens when we don't use discretion. Once your words are out of the bag, they can end up anywhere.

Within departments there are always politics. I can't tell you how many times key people have tried to get me to talk about my views on things. They've tried to get information. I am learning to keep my opinions to myself because my views will be read as my husband's views. And that could get him into hot water.

When you are socializing with people from the department, play out beforehand what you will disclose and not disclose. You don't ever have to be rude unless someone gets out of line. Smile. But be careful about passing along information that could jeopardize the well being of your husband. Better yet, stay clear of controversial work topics and share about the other aspects of your lives.

Someone Older and Wiser

Renee's husband, Joel, had been deployed to Iraq twice. When his time was up with the National Guard, he went to work for the sheriff's department. Renee had struggled deeply with little kids in tow while he was in the Middle East. She felt very alone, and there wasn't much support available. Those years were very hard. So when Joel came home and became a cop, she was glad that he was home, but there were still stresses with his job.

About that time she met a woman who was also a deputy wife. Cyndi was a little older, and her husband had been with the county for several years. She took a liking to Renee, and they soon found they had much in common. Soon this friendship blossomed into a mentoring relationship. Cyndi called Renee from time to time and asked her how she was faring. She'd answer questions and listened to Renee's concerns. She gently guided Renee to keep on investing in her marriage and children and offered understanding and helpful ideas. Unlike the lonely deployment experience, she felt supported and strong.

I, too, have benefited from mentoring relationships. When I was younger, I sought out confident women that I respected and asked them to meet with me for guidance. The time was invaluable. I sat soaking in tried and true wisdom and remember much of what they said all these years later.

In recent years I have been able to pay it forward. I am now a mentor to several ladies and feel honored that younger women want to meet with me. I love listening and sharing wisdom and asking questions to get them to really think about the deep stuff.

If this kind of a friendship appeals to you, start looking for a seasoned woman from the office or another department. It helps if she is a law enforcement wife, but it doesn't have to necessarily be so. Look for a wise, quiet yet confident woman who cares about you and

Victoria M. Newman

your marriage. Then take the plunge and ask her to meet regularly.

Him Too!

Up to this point I have talked about getting support from others. But I cannot move ahead without mentioning the most influential person of your support system: your husband! You are one entity, and you can lean on one another. Two lives intertwined, investing time, resources, and parts of yourselves to build a life together.

A long-term marriage is a journey of growth. I mentioned earlier that Brent and I had spent our earlier years peeling off our rough edges so that we can enjoy our soft centers in the later years. To be able to do this takes a two-way give and take, not a one-sided approach. Some of your needs will only be met by him.

Your husband's input and support is valuable no matter how hard it may be to hear. Our guys many times will be brutally honest; they've been trained to call it like they see it. For many women this is hard to take.

Kim didn't see James as her protector for many years. Every time she brought her unresolved conflicts to him from work, he'd ask questions about her response. He was never quick to join her pity parties and didn't seem to take her side much. He was painfully objective. After awhile Kim translated that to mean that he didn't care enough to protect her.

But James had a different approach. His support was unwavering for Kim, but he had a whole-picture viewpoint. Rather than take her side no matter what, he thought it best to counsel her to see the situation not as a victim but as an involved party. Sometimes Kim would be right but not always. James felt she should take responsibility for her part in problems, not just enable the victim mentality she resorted to. As Kim matured over the years, she came to see that James was no doubt a protector—he protected her dignity.

Your husband can support you even if he doesn't see things your way. In fact, it is always better to get another opinion that is different from your own and then think it through. Our husbands are trained to ask good questions and think objectively. Generally women are led by emotions of compassion and empathy as well as a healthy need for significance. But these strong emotions can sometimes trick us. We may not be able to see the full picture. Our husbands can add in other thoughts that help balance us out, and vice versa. They are a strong addition to our support system.

Time for Reinforcement

Andy and Karen were struggling to make ends meet on their police department salary. Andy was working graveyard shift and tried to pick up extra shifts to give them a little breathing room financially. Karen was growing more and more discontent with never seeing her husband, which led to anger. She was almost ready to call it quits when they went to talk with a pastor at their church. After listening to their plight, he suggested counseling. But they were already strapped financially and couldn't afford it. He then suggested that they meet with another law enforcement couple who could provide some counsel and guidance. Because they'd heard Brent and I speak at a law enforcement function, they contacted us.

We met for a year or so, first as couples then individually. We were able to come alongside them and help them to talk through their issues in a condemnation-free environment. We didn't offer much advice unless they asked for it but brought up pieces of problems they should look at and discuss. They were soon back on track, but we continue to keep in contact with them to make sure they're solid.

Sometimes we need a little help to get past the obstacles we face in our marriages. Finding other people who can help you in some way is another piece of your support system. Mentoring and marriage retreats can be a great way to invest in your relationship, as can counseling.

Erica and Marlo, mentioned in previous chapters, go to counseling regularly, like dental check ups. They need a little cleaning to keep things healthy. Others go only when they are in crisis. But do your homework. Not all counselors are created equal. Try to get some recommendations. Inquire if they work with law enforcement. If you are of a particular faith, you may want to ensure that the counselor's approach is compatible with your beliefs. Spend time in the research beforehand and have their information available for when you need it.

Counsel, friendships with women, your relationship with your husband, and other members of law enforcement all make up your support system. You can't do life alone and remain healthy. We need each other for the ups and for the downs.

Discussion Group Questions

1. Who is the one who supports you the best? Give an example.

2. Which of the four rules of friendship did you like to see? Why?

3. Spend the rest of your time brainstorming some events that you all would like to do together. Follow through!

Victoria M. Newman

Chapter 8:
Stuff Happens: When Hard Times Come

Because my husband has PTSD from his deployment to Iraq, the Fourth of July is now about renting loud movies, closing all the windows and blinds or praying that he gets called into work so he can be barricaded behind the prison walls where the outside can't come in. I don't fully understand it all, but that's what we have to do now to make him feel better. We help relieve some of his anxieties and reassure him that while he will never forget what he went through, God is still taking the time to heal his heart and mind. We do it one day, one step, and one prayer at a time.

Renee, wife of former National Guardsman
and current sheriff's deputy

You may have heard the tongue-in-cheek phrase about motorcycle cops: "They say there are two kinds of motors: those who've gone down and those who will go down." It's a little along the lines of a law enforcement career in general: those who have had some kind of difficulty on the job and those who will. In a twenty-to-thirty-year career, your man will suffer something. Injuries, long-term effects of hypervigilance, supervisors who don't get it, burnout, post-traumatic stress disorder (PTSD), grief over fallen comrades and other difficulties will at some point take a toll. How will you maneuver through these challenges together?

There are three kinds of stress that law enforcement officers experience. The first is general stress, the day-to-day things that life hands us. There are varying levels depending on the seasons that we go through—illness, death of a loved one, financial pressures, and so on.

The second kind of stress that your spouse may go through is cumulative stress. Dr. Ellen Kirschman describes cumulative stress as "prolonged, unrelieved wear and tear that results from having more demands than a person can respond to."[11] This is also called burnout.

The third kind of stress is critical incident stress. This develops when a specific event happens that overwhelms the officer's ability to cope effectively. Examples would include accidents that have multiple fatalities or that involve children, a mass casualty incident (like 9/11), a shooting, a suicide of a co-worker, and other disturbing incidents.

Some of the symptoms of critical incident stress are physical. These include chest pain, trouble breathing, trembling, high blood pressure, stomach issues, headaches, fatigue, and poor sleep. Emotional symptoms include denial, fear, depression, feelings of helplessness or feeling overwhelmed, anger, and excessive dwelling on the event. Other symptoms of critical incident stress are cognitive. These include disorientation, hyper-alertness, issues with concentration and memory, nightmares and flashbacks, and assigning blame to others. There are other responses reflected in behavior. In addition to some that I go into a bit more below, you may see changes in eating habits, crying spells, and unusual spending.

As wives, we need to be aware of the ways our men respond to stress and learn to recognize problems. It's not an if; it's when. Life happens. I've provided information on some responses to job stress. It is not an exhaustive list. If you suspect that any of these areas are affecting your guy, I would suggest you do a little extra research of your own so that you can support him in an educated manner.

The One That Sticks with Him

Rick was the toughest cop in the room. He'd been on the force for a quarter of a century and had earned respect among his peers. He prided himself in the fact that he kept it together. But there was always a picture in the back of his mind of a little girl and her father that burned to death while he was helpless to save them because of the intensity of the fire. For twenty years he kept it inside until my husband asked him the right question.

The tears spilled and made room for relief. He'd never even told his wife that he attended the little girl's funeral. And for years it ate at him. When he was ready, he let it go in the presence of several of his fellow coworkers. It was a powerful moment for all who were in attendance.

There will be incidents that, for whatever reason, will insert themselves into our husbands' minds and sear the images on their hearts. There will be pain, maybe even sorrow. And, depending on your husband's ability to cope with it, they could do some damage. For some officers, stuffing incidents like this will result in PTSD years after the fact.

Anger

I met Tami by chance at a baseball game. We got to talking and learned that we were both married to police officers. When I told her I was writing a book, she shrugged and said she had another book she was supposed to be reading. I recognized the book and thought it was very helpful to me, but she seemed to begrudge it. I asked why.

"I don't want to read anything that gives him an excuse for bad behavior," she replied. We plunged into a discussion as to what she was experiencing. She disclosed that her husband had anger issues. He would rant and rave at her and the kids and feel better afterward, so no apology. She and the kids were suffering. She then mentioned that it started when her kids became teenagers.

My educated guess was that her husband was feeling out of control with his teenagers. Younger children are easier to lead into obedience. They are more impressionable and tend to want to please their parents. But teenagers struggle to find their identity and are looking for their own independence. Some will fight back or disobey altogether. They are much harder to control.

Meanwhile Tami's husband has been trained to be in control of all situations. If there are people who don't respond to him, he has been trained to force them to comply. He was bringing home that training. His frustration at not being able to control his teenagers gave way to the explosive anger.

David Augsburger, in his book *Caring Enough to Confront* says this:

> "Underneath my feelings of anger—there are concealed expectations. (I may not yet be aware of them myself.) Inside my angry statements – there are hidden demands. (I may not yet be able to put them into words.) Until I deal with the demands, I am doing little about it all.
>
> "Anger may be the demand that you hear me or that you recognize my worth, or that you see me as precious and worthy to be loved, or that you respect me, let go of my arm, or quit trying to take control of my life."[12]

If your husband is dealing with anger, remember that anger is a demand for something. A soft answer from you may help to bring the situation to a calmer level. You can talk out some of his demands/expectations in quieter moments and help him to see what it is that he expects. When you both understand these expectations, you can work toward working through it together.

Augsburger also says, "Explosive anger is powerless to effect change in relationships …Vented anger may ventilate feelings and provide instant though temporary release for tortured emotions, but it does little for relationships.

"Clearly expressed anger, however, is something different. Clear statements of anger feelings and angry demands can slice through emotional barriers or communication tangles to establish contact."[13]

Anger is a tricky thing. Appropriate anger to express demands is helpful to move along conflict resolution. Explosive anger isn't helpful; in fact, it could be harmful. Linda and John had been married for several years. When they would have an argument, she would resort to yelling. Over time, her anger escalated into hitting, and it continued for years. One night she hit him several times, and he'd had enough. He called the police, and she was arrested for domestic abuse. Linda spent the next two days in jail. Fortunately, it was the wake up call she needed. "My time in jail was very sobering," Linda recounts. "On the ceiling directly above my head were the words, 'God will make a way.' It spoke to me like nothing ever has. It took years and was

Victoria M. Newman

very difficult to reconcile the events of that evening. But not only have we resumed our relationship more peacefully, we are incredibly close and our relationship has grown leaps and bounds. It truly took this all to happen to find peace and to be grateful for the trials that make us stronger. The anger I was feeling toward Brian had nothing to do with him...it was all me and what I needed to deal with. He was just a safe target, or so it seemed."

While this story has had a productive outcome, many cases of spousal abuse do not. Don't let your or your spouse's anger escalate to the point of harm. And if it happens, get help immediately.

Substance Abuse

Alcohol and drug dependence are coping mechanisms. Something is up, and they have developed a crutch to lean on. Here are some symptoms of a drinking problem, adapted from Alcoholics Anonymous:

1. You have tried to stop drinking for a set amount of time and couldn't go the distance.

2. You want people to quit telling you to quit drinking.

3. You switched from one kind of alcohol to another to avoid getting drunk.

4. You need a drink to get started on the day or to stop shaking.

5. You envy people who don't get themselves into trouble while drinking.

6. You've had problems related to your drinking in the past year.

7. Your drinking is causing problems at home.

8. You try to get extra drinks at a party because what is served is not enough.

9. You tell yourself you could stop drinking any time but keep getting drunk without meaning to.

10. You've missed work or school because of your drinking.

11. You have blackouts, times when drinking that you don't remember.

12. You feel like your life would be better if you didn't drink.

If you suspect that your guy has a drinking problem, talk with him about it when he isn't drinking. Be ready with specific examples of behavior, not generalized accusations. If he denies it, get others involved who love your husband. Have your resources lined up—phone numbers, locations of meetings and support groups, and people to contact.

Victoria M. Newman

PTSD

Brenda's husband had nightmares and suffered uncontrollable shaking. Rhonda's husband told her he was sure he was crazy and even acted like it sometimes. Mary's husband retreated to the fetal position on the couch and whimpered like a baby then later left her for someone else. All of these men were diagnosed with PTSD.

Post-traumatic stress disorder is a condition that results from a critical incident or develops as a result of repeated exposure to trauma, both very frequent in the career of a police officer. In his book *CopShock, Second Edition: Surviving Post-traumatic Stress Disorder* Allen Kates says that "one in three cops may suffer from PTSD, a condition that could lead to depression, suicidal thoughts, addictions, eating disorders as well as job and family conflict."[14] Some of the common symptoms include anger, nightmares, flashbacks, concentration problems, emotional detachment, and avoidance of people and places.

The Power of a Good Marriage

It was a perfect day for Clarke and Tracie to chill out in the pool. But Clarke felt like he would sink beneath the weight of dread. He was struggling with the stuff he'd seen on duty. He wasn't thinking he'd kill himself, but knew he was starting to head down that road, and he needed help. He'd inwardly argued with himself for quite awhile before he took the plunge. "This stuff is gettin' to me, Trace. I'm not okay." As soon as it left his mouth, the weight lifted. Until she replied in horror, "Are you kidding me?!" It was not the response he was looking for.

On the outside, Clarke was supercop. On the inside, a teen's suicide triggered a breaking point. "It was one of five suicides that day, and it was my boiling point," explains Clarke. "Everything began haunting me. Everything came out—calls from the day before, the week before, the year before, ten years before. They all came back and they came back with a vengeance. Everything I thought I had dealt with, but really just disassociated from, came back."

He'd told himself to get over it, forget it. But when he couldn't, he decided he was a coward—a loser. But he did have a great relationship with his wife, and he trusted her enough to share his pain. And although initially her response was less than ideal, by the end of the day she understood that he did the most courageous thing he could've ever done—ask for help. After doing some research together, they found the assistance he needed.

Clarke and Tracie are now hosting police suicide prevention seminars across the country. As part of his healing, Clarke made a movie called "The Pain Behind the Badge," and it's speaking to officers who have suffered silently for years. When Tracie gets up to speak, she imparts these powerful words: "Why did I ever think he was okay after twenty-two years on the job?

Victoria M. Newman

The Rock of Gibraltar was crumbling, and I never saw it coming. I'm lucky he's alive."

Post-traumatic stress disorder can be very serious, but there is help available. See the resources in the back of this book to consider avenues of restoring health to your officer.

Fifteen Is Enough!

A few years back, Brent and I were getting ready for bed at the end of the day when he checked his Blackberry one last time. Another suicide. It was number fifteen for our department in a period of four years. I cried out, "Another one?! What are we *doing*?!" I didn't know it at the time, but it was quite a prophetic question. I was referring to the department—how will they respond? But actually the more I asked the question, I realized that I might be able to do something as well.

I don't know what it was about the number fifteen, but it seemed like everyone jumped into action. Number fifteen pushed the panic button, and we awoke. The department began talking about suicide openly. Our officers' association published a double-page ad in their monthly newsletter: "Call for Backup," with a picture of a glass of alcohol and a gun. We implemented awareness seminars across the state and set up debriefing sessions with those who knew the suicide victims. We educated ourselves. We decided as a department to hit suicide head on, deal with it as the reality it was, not a deniable secret hovering in the shadows.

In my own research, I learned that almost always the one who commits suicide just ended a significant relationship. When a life is going sideways, others are affected in a big way. Helplessness, blame, an inability to get a handle on problems, and depression (among other things) will push away those who are close. When things are falling apart, and hope seems to have been lost, the natural tendency is to get out quickly. The boat is sinking, and our survival instincts say, "Abandon ship!" Sometimes this is one more reason for those contemplating suicide.

This book is part of my own action against suicide. I care about the mental and emotional health of my husband and those he works alongside. If by sharing my own struggles I can encourage other wives to hang tough through the hard stuff, maybe suicide won't be such an attractive option to their officers. If educating law enforcement spouses about these realities equips them to deal positively with the negatives, then perhaps marriages will be saved. If our officers know they have backup at home, perhaps they will be more courageous to get the help they need.

Symptoms of Suicide

So how can we discern if our spouse is contemplating suicide? By watching and listening for the symptoms. Sometimes there are signs of PTSD, whether from one specific incident, or a collection of events over time. If they don't deal with the trauma, they risk depression, which can be a precursor to suicide. If your officer is having trouble reconciling these thoughts, he may be at risk. According to several articles on police suicide, a typical profile of a suicide candidate is a white male, 35 years of age, separated or divorced, using alcohol or drugs, and having recently experienced a loss or disappointment. They may have made out a recent will, bought a weapon, or appear to be getting their affairs in order. There is generally a significant mood change—either better or worse. They may exhibit signs of anxiety, frustration, or confusion.

I once heard suicide referred to as a permanent solution to a temporary problem. But in the midst of it, the problem *seems* permanent. Sometimes it takes another level head to discern what is going on in the big picture. This is where you come in. Learn to recognize the symptoms. If your officer seems like he's at risk, don't abandon him or ignore the symptoms. Fight for him! Find help immediately.

How to Deal with His Crisis

Whatever crises our husbands undergo, they need us, and they need us to be strong. Depending on the circumstances, we could be the ones who are there for them to talk out some of the emotion. But when it's too big for us, we can come alongside and love them enough to get them the help they need. Whatever they are dealing with, they need to know they aren't alone.

Our husbands, however, may not want to be "fixed." It's their deal, and they want to work it out. In this situation, perhaps they don't understand the effects on us and our children. Maybe ego is a factor. Maybe they have adopted a cultural view that police officers are supposed to be tough and not show weakness. Sometimes they need space to work out the answer rather than depending on us too much.

Depending on your husband's department, there may be a stigma against bringing up stress. In some cases, doing so may jeopardize their career. For many years, the culture of law enforcement has been to ignore responses to trauma. These responses have been labeled as weakness. Fortunately, the thinking within law enforcement circles is gradually changing into thinking that trauma is a natural response to the unnatural incidents that our cops experience. While this new way of thinking is slowly making its way throughout the country, it isn't yet universal. If this is the case for your husband, he'll need a safe listener, and it may need to be you.

There are three stages of dealing with his crisis. First, identify the problem beneath the symptoms. Seek the cause to the effect. I've listed some things here, but this is by no means all there is. Do some research online. Talk with a seasoned wife or another officer you trust. If your department does have resources, by all means take advantage of them.

There are a few practical things you can do as his wife while dealing with his crisis:

Victoria M. Newman

- Create a safe place to come home to. Be ready to listen without judgment or fearful reaction. Spend good, quality time with him in his off-duty time.

- Make an appointment for him to get a physical. Stress can take a toll on his body. Nip health problems in the bud.

- As much as you can, create delicious, healthy meals for your family. Stress tends to increase a desire for junk.

- Discourage making important decisions when he is overwhelmed.

- Maintain normalcy with life. Routine can keep balance in the midst of trials.

- Write down your feelings through the journey. When you're on the other side, you can look back and see how far you both have come.

Second, deal with it head on. It is so important for us as wives to support them in a way that is not codependent. We want to understand and support them as our husbands, but that doesn't mean making excuses for their behavior. If there is a problem, treat it as reality and work toward a solution. If it's an issue like burnout he's dealing with, that could be easily identified and worked through without professionals. But if it's bigger and deeper, seek help.

Resources Available

Talk with someone safe. Find out if your husband's department has programs designed to help in each of these issues. If so, make sure that there is confidentiality and then proceed. A police chaplaincy program is another potentially valuable resource. There are many avenues of crisis intervention, and they are designed to discreetly come alongside.

Check if your department has an employee assistance program. They are designed to help police officers get the help they need, sometimes even paying for counseling. Inquire if your husband's department has a peer support program where other officers have gone through something similar, and join with your loved one to help them through the recovery process. Some departments also offer support groups for related issues.

Religious communities and organizations throughout the country and abroad have many different resources as well. Counseling, support groups and programs, books, and radio programs are designed to come alongside and provide encouragement, support, and guidance.

If these avenues have been tried, and still your officer is struggling, consider an intensive retreat. Two facilities exist in the United States to treat problems related to PTSD and critical incident stress. In California there is the West Coast Post-trauma Retreat. The On-Site Academy is located in Massachusetts. These three- to five-day retreats are held monthly and are designed to help emergency personnel who are overwhelmed by a critical incident or other job-related trauma. The resources section at the back of this book contains contact information.

Through these resources, build your support system. Don't hesitate if you feel your man is in trouble. His life and your marriage depend on it.

Take Time to Recover

The third stage is to take time to recover. Try to get some time off and get away for a change of scenery. Build positive memories. Take a break from extra-curricular activities that create more busyness. Make sure your family gets rest. If your relationship is at a relational deficit, then start making deposits.

This is also a good time to set some new boundaries relating to the issue. Perhaps you both need to stop spending time with friends who drink heavily and find other avenues for friendship. Maybe you both need to set some boundaries with activities that aggravate issues. Follow the avenues of healthy support. You also have the unique position to help him get the nourishment he needs through healthy meals and exercise. In fact, eating right and exercising are essential for his (and your) healing.

What I'm suggesting here is for the both of you. His crisis affects you in a huge way. Things you go through affect him as well because your lives are intertwined. You both need time to recover and to heal. In some cases it could be a lengthy road. You'll need this time to remain patient while the problems are resolved.

Being Strong When We Feel Weak

Years ago the mentor I met with while a newlywed was diagnosed with an aggressive brain tumor. Debbie was given six months to live but died in five. During that time I too was dealing with internal hurts that needed healing. It was really tough. A wise friend of mine encouraged me to watch for what I could learn during this time. "Find purpose in the pain," she said. I'd never done that before, and in the midst of it all, it seemed impossible.

But it wasn't. With the help and support of my husband, eventually I viewed the end of Debbie's life as a new beginning for me. Debbie had imparted a bit of her heart into mine, and this I could hold on to. Incredibly, the final piece of my healing was put into place through a conversation at her funeral. And although I miss her even now, in a way I keep Debbie alive as I carry forward what she taught me.

When you are going through painful seasons of life, challenge yourself. Try to find purpose amidst the pain. What can you learn? What can you carry forward? How can you have victory over what seems like defeat?

When life is topsy-turvy, we need to be held up by our foundations and support system (see chapters six and seven). There may be a tendency to withdraw when things are tough, but it is when we need others

Victoria M. Newman

all the more. A timely phone call or a meal provided is very uplifting. You never know what kindnesses others will offer when you are in crisis.

As a person of faith, I turn to God for comfort. He has been my refuge and strength in the midst of some very hard times.

The last bit of help may just come from your own attitude. It may sound strange, but when you are going through tough times, be thankful. Sometimes you might have to start with being thankful your situation isn't worse than it is! It may seem like your life is in shambles, but there is always something small (or large) to be thankful for. You will be surprised how being grateful will lift your spirits!

How Do You Spell Relief?

Whether the issues that you face in your marriage are a result of his job or relational differences or other outside pressures, there is a likelihood that at some point you will want to give up. Even the best marriages have occasional long winter seasons, and we are human.

For sixteen months, Brent lived out of town during the week while he commanded another area. Then he transferred to a local position but took on the most challenging job of his life. I saw him more, but for the first few months he came home and promptly fell asleep on the couch. His job took more and more of his energy, concentration, and time. Then personal hard times hit. It was very difficult. After many months of

HOW TO LOVE YOUR COP WITH ATTITUDE

seemingly impossible demands at work and at home, I saw a change in his behavior. He became withdrawn, angry, forgetful, and, at times, almost victim-like. This wasn't like him. For awhile, I was concerned for him. But then I became more concerned about me.

"How long will this last?" led to "I don't want to be treated like this," which led to "I don't deserve this." That led to "I don't have to take this anymore!"

I started detaching myself, entertaining thoughts of escape. It became a big temptation that consumed several days a week. I stopped fighting for us in my mind. I was letting go, giving up. With each squabble and each let-down, I found myself drifting farther and farther away and hurting more and more.

It was the first time in our marriage that I considered leaving. It was a very strong temptation. Frankly I just wanted out. I needed relief.

We took a vacation to the beach in southern California, and I wondered how to tell him where I was. We bumped along through the week, and I felt so distant. He was in the same room, but I felt we'd grown miles apart. One day we took a trip to the zoo with the kids. As we got into the car, we had an argument, and that was the final straw. All the way home it was over for me. I'd had enough. I didn't want this anymore.

After dinner I went for a walk on the beach to clear my head. As I walked toward the ocean, I noticed a really cool sandcastle that someone had built that day. It was fortified with thick little towers around it and stones and a moat. Someone spent a lot of time building it.

Victoria M. Newman

The tide was coming in. A wave lapped at the fortress that surrounded it, and suddenly I was riveted. For the next hour, I watched as wave after wave washed bits of the castle away. The fortress was the first to go. Then the waves methodically carved a hole in the back side of the castle I couldn't see. Suddenly the top fell off, and the waves washed it away within minutes. Then a large wave swept up, and the rest of the castle split in half. My chest tightened, and I caught a sob. My eyes filled with tears as I realized that, to me, it was not a sandcastle disappearing but my own home.

I heard a whisper: "Are you gonna do this to your family?"

I wept as the tide completely wiped the sandcastle away, leaving only the stones that garnished the fortress. It was as if it had never existed. And I heard that still, small, but firm voice ask me again, "Are you going to do this to Brent? To your kids? Everything you've built will be for nothing. And for what?"

I looked up at the blurred stars through my tear-filled eyes. "No," I decided, "No, I cannot do this. No! I will not leave."

I listened to the waves crashing on the shore and gained a little strength.

"No, I will not do this to my husband. I will not destroy my family."

The hurt still burned in my heart. But I decided to stay. And then I decided to recommit myself to loving my husband no matter what he was going through.

After that night I had to re-train my mind to think positively about Brent and our relationship. It took a couple weeks, but then I realized that he was hurting too. He was burnt out. He was empty, weary, and he needed me! So I reached out with a new attitude and started actively loving him again even though not much changed on his end at first. I loved him first out of compassion but then with fervency.

Then things began to change. He relaxed. Work seemed to ease up. We started laughing together. Twenty days after the sandcastle moment, he presented me with a beautiful little song that he had heard and thought it could be ours. This meant so much to me! It seemed that once I decided to stay, my recommitment encouraged him and lifted him out of the place he was in.

Think We, Not Me

As I look back, I realize that I let myself get really self-focused. It became more about me than we. And when times are tough, this is a recipe for failure.

That night on the beach reminded me of something else. After the sandcastle disappeared, I looked to my right and saw some large rocks that some condominiums were built upon. I realized that Brent and I had built our relationship on a strong foundation of trust, mutual respect, and unconditional love. We were undergoing some strong storms of life and had been pelted and worn down. But because our foundation

Victoria M. Newman

was strong, we would not fail. Our life together would not disappear like a castle built on sand; it would stand the test of time.

Discussion Group Questions

1.   Describe a time in which your husband struggled with his job. How did you deal with it?

2.   Talk about ways you have come up with to ease his stress.

3.   Next week bring copies of your favorite healthy recipe.

4.   Share something you learned from a difficult time in your life.

Chapter 9:
Silver Bullets:
Money and Your Marriage

Don't even consider keeping up with the Joneses. THEY'RE BROKE!

The number one cause of divorce in North America is stress due to money problems.

Dave Ramsey, financial advisor

It's no secret. Across the country and beyond, we're vulnerable to economic trends. Why? Because, for most of us, we are dependent upon other people's money. We have become increasingly dependent on Wall Street, banks, and the government. We work hard, and then everyone takes a cut. Then we get to choose how to spend the leftovers. If we decide that the leftovers aren't enough, we borrow. Pretty soon our choices are made for us; we no longer have enough left over from the leftovers to live. It's a vicious cycle, and we've seen the consequences of this in the last few years. People are losing their homes, jobs, and more. Cop families are no different.

Carl and Tina declared bankruptcy and lost their gorgeous house because they bought whatever they wanted on credit and then couldn't pay the mortgage.

Quinn and Saul both work just to make ends meet because half of Saul's salary goes to alimony payments.

Brian and Marcy depended on his overtime to make their house payment. It severely cut back Brian's opportunities to expand professionally, and he was hardly home with his family.

Carrie and Andy bought an expensive house on the outreaches of what they could afford. Then the police department implemented a pay cut. She ended up having to teach school when she desperately wanted to be home with her little girls.

All of these families are law enforcement. Good careers. Excellent benefits. Decent salaries. But no matter how much money is made, failure to plan is a plan for failure.

The Role of Hypervigilance

There are law enforcement-related issues that affect our money. Hypervigilance and critical incident stress have their effects. Dr. Gilmartin says,

> The behavioral and marketing researchers on Madison Avenue have... clearly established that certain individuals, when feeling mildly depressed or unfocused, can find themselves

HOW TO LOVE YOUR COP WITH ATTITUDE

feeling more energetic if they purchase something. This form of "retail therapy" does have distinct gender differences. Women tend to make small ticket purchases... Males do not appear to like to go shopping, but they do enjoy "buying stuff"... big-ticket items like boats, cars, pickup trucks, motor homes, campers, and maybe some power tools.[15]

What happens is that retail therapy can turn into debt. And debt becomes a huge burden that results in extra jobs and overtime. The catch phrase "he who has the most toys wins" turns into "he who has the most toys whines."

This spending pattern affects our marriages. More and more debt is added to our limited resources and can rob us of financial security. We are constantly behind, working harder and harder to catch up. Dr. Gilmartin adds,

> This cycle robs the officer of any sense of financial security across the span of the occupational career. Many officers, without having a sense of proactive control of their finances, experience significant distress economically, in spite of enjoying an occupational career that is generally free of lay-offs and downsizing, with excellent retirement and medical benefits.

One of the benefits of police work is the financial security it brings to the family. Most sworn police officers are in it for the long haul; a twenty-to-thirty year career in law enforcement is the goal. There are exceptions, but depending on what your department offers in pay and benefits, chances are good that you'll belong to the middle class. Also, law enforcement is a reasonably secure profession. There will always be crime; therefore, we will always need police officers.

But if we allow ourselves to get into debt to the point that we are strapped financially, that feeling of security begins to wane. When our officers are working day in and day out but money is constantly coming up short, a sense of frustration can develop. These feelings will heap on top of regular pressures of the job, and can lead to a feeling of desperation. At this point, talking about money will become very difficult.

Money Talks

Ted and Sarah have difficulty talking about money, as it is a constant source of conflict. Ted gets frustrated that he works hard to bring in the money and they never seem to get ahead. Sarah naturally avoids conflict, so she inadvertently sabotages their efforts by not communicating with Ted about upcoming bills. This of course angers Ted and adds late charges to an already tight budget.

Even though money seems like it should be handled without emotion, it isn't. So much of who we are is wrapped up in our money! For men the traditional role as provider says a lot about who they are as a man.

Victoria M. Newman

The expectations have been built up into status. If you make a lot of money, you are a success. If you don't, not so much!

For women, we tend to view money as security. If we have money, we don't have to worry about where to live, what we wear, and what we eat. If we are short on money, we tend to worry.

Rich and Anna didn't have a large income, but they made it work. However, Rich felt that because he worked hard he deserved a nice truck. He spent a lot of money on his trucks while Anna scrimped and saved and did odd jobs to feed and clothe the kids. Over the years Anna and Rich had many arguments, and eventually Anna took over the management of the money. She didn't give Rich much to spend, so when Rich got an overtime check, he'd cash it and spend it without telling her.

How you handle money can build trust or be a source of mistrust. Typically, every couple has a spender and a saver. And unless the two have agreed upon goals and budgets, the constant push and pull of the money can be destructive to a marriage. The solution lies in acknowledging our shortcomings and for both to be involved in money management. We need to ask ourselves the hard questions and then answer honestly:

- Are we both committed to improving this area?

- Who is the saver, who is the spender?

- What are our individual responsibilities?

- What do we both want from our money?

- Where can we cut our spending to invest in our future?

- When do we waver in our control of spending?

- How did we get ourselves into the debt we have? How will we get out?

- Are we a slave to our home, striving to make the payments?

- Is our money working for us, or against us?

- How deep are we willing to cut luxuries to ease financial stress?

Have a regular business meeting with your husband to get on top of things. When we are proactive about communicating, especially when it comes to money, it will have an accumulating effect much like the emotional bank account. For the one who does most of the money business, it'll really help him/you feel a lighter burden.

To keep our money life intact, we need some guiding principles. Then we need a plan based on those principles. I've included some financial guidelines that Brent and I have learned and tried to practice over the years.

Victoria M. Newman

Keep Your Money Life Intact

- Spend less than you earn. This should be a no-brainer, but most people just don't adhere to this idea. When I was a newlywed, my boss told me, "You should live on Brent's salary and save yours." I thought he was nuts. But I will tell you it was the best advice we never followed. Had we taken his advice, we would've been in much better shape early on.

- Debt is a four-letter word. When we don't save and pay cash for items other than a mortgage, we will pay much more for what we buy. Sales prices will quickly be added to in a hurry. Why do you think we get discounts for using credit at department stores? The odds are in their favor that we won't be able to pay it off before we incur interest.

- Budget, budget, budget! This is the only way we can live within our means. We have found that the best way to do this is through a software program. There are many programs from which to choose. Do a Google search and you'll have more information than you ever dreamed. We have successfully used Quicken for years, but there are other programs that may offer options that are better suited to your situation. We can pay bills, budget, keep track of what we spend, and even download our spending into TurboTax, making tax time just a little easier.

- The 10-10-80 spending plan. Ten percent goes to savings. Ten percent goes toward giving to charity. Budget and spend the rest. My daughter is excellent at this plan. When she started babysitting at twelve years of age, she put together a spreadsheet on the computer that charted her progress. She's been faithful to it ever since. She gave 10 percent to our church and other needy causes, then put 60 percent into her savings, and spent 30 percent on fun stuff. She was able to do this because we were taking care of her needs. Once she became an adult and is now taking on more financial responsibility, she has new percentages that include her car and school expenses. But even now she still gives 10 percent to charity and 20 percent to savings.

- Don't spend; invest. Typically we look at money as something we spend rather than a tool used to invest in our futures. When we have this slightly different perspective, we tend to be more proactive in proceeding wisely with our money. When we have goals and dreams for our futures and then view our money as the means to meet them, we are much less likely to let our money slip through our fingers.

Victoria M. Newman

It Can Be Better

Are we destined to always struggle with our money? How much is enough? Will there ever be enough? Like Ted, does your husband feel the pressure of providing for the family yet feel as if the debt gets bigger as the hopes grow smaller to ever reach your goals? If so you're not alone. Unlike most relational things, there actually is a formula to solve our financial woes.

I recently heard two cop wives talking about their finances. They were both on the same money plan and were comparing notes.

"Where are you in the process?" asked Barbara.

"We are now debt-free, except for the mortgage," Eve said with a smile.

"Wow! That was quick!"

"We had a lot of things to sell," explained Eve, "Then we took the money and paid off debt. We found a renter for our big house, and now we have a down payment on a smaller home in a better community. It's all been working out very well. We don't have to count on Ben's overtime anymore. How about you?"

"We have about a year and a half, and we'll be debt free. We've whittled our expenses down to the point that we have extra money each month that goes toward paying off our credit cards. It is so freeing!"

The plan that Barbara and Eve were speaking of is Dave Ramsay's "Total Money Makeover." His book of the same name shares a simple yet smart plan to get out of debt as soon as possible and then use your money to build wealth in smart ways. Brent and I took a money class shortly after we were married. The class was called *Master Your Money*, by Ron Blue. We learned some great principles for managing our finances. More recently we read Ramsay's book together. His ideas and principles were very timely.

Whether you choose Dave Ramsay, Ron Blue, or something else, the point is to have an agreed upon plan. If you are currently in a difficult place financially, there is hope. Get creative. It's amazing to watch your money make the shift from burden to delight as you get spending under control and see it grow. It'll be one more thing under control in your law enforcement life. And that makes a huge difference!

Bonus!

Once our oldest daughter was born, I quit work and stayed home with our children. It was reducing to one income that forced us to pinch pennies. We had mouths to feed and only so much money to buy that food. I've listed some ways that we have implemented to bring down our costs.

- Get out of debt; interest should be the first expense to go.

- Pay your bills on time; late fees should not be a budget item.

Victoria M. Newman

- Have your paycheck direct deposited; many times banks will waive a monthly service charge if you do this.

- Raise your insurance deductibles as high as you can comfortably go; this will bring down your premiums. Then make sure you have the deductible in savings.

- Turn off the lights when you leave the room, unplug appliances after use, and turn off computers at night. Use extra freezers or refrigerators only when entertaining.

- Shop at discount stores and warehouses. Split large quantities with friends.

- Go without meat a couple of nights a week for dinner. Have pasta with marinara or salads or soups. Rice and beans are a great supper with complete protein and no expensive cuts of meat.

- Buy juice from a can and mix in your own water. You can save as much as 150 percent on the cost.

- You would be surprised at the beautiful clothes you can find at thrift shops. I have several friends who dress beautifully from thrift shop deals. You'd never know.

- If you're an avid reader, borrow fiction from the library or friends or buy used books.

Only buy books new that you will refer to again (like this book).

- Cut back on newspapers and magazine subscriptions. Renew only those you read regularly. Listen to news on the radio; you can multitask, and it's free!

- Make your own coffee. Buy the good stuff: it's still cheaper to make.

- Make your own lunch. Buy the good deli meat: it's still cheaper to make.

- Make sure you don't buy extra roadside assistance if your auto insurance already offers this. You'd be surprised how many people do this!

- Grow a garden. Nowadays gardens can even be grown in pots on the patio.

- Do indoor dates with homemade popcorn, a video, and a glass of wine after the kids have gone to bed. You'll save a small fortune and won't drink and drive.

- Use coupons for restaurants!

- Rather than eat in, take it to go. You save on drinks and tip. Have the kids share entrees to cut down on waste.

- Do your shopping on the Internet; there are always better prices. Watch for waived shipping costs and sales to get the best possible deal. Brent pays a yearly fee for two-day shipping through Amazon.com, and they don't charge tax. Saves us plenty.

- Look for bundle packages on media. Cell phone service, cable, and landline service companies will sometimes work together to reduce your monthly bills.

- If you have teenagers, pay the monthly flat rate for texting. It'll save you money, guaranteed. And it'll save on your minutes.

- Always ask your husband if he knows coworkers with side businesses. Cops will many times give cops a good deal. It's kind of a co-op thing.

- Inquire whether your union has concierge services. You can save money on vacations and amusement parks among other things.

These are some of the savings I have found when trying to balance the budget. They are tried and true.

Money is a huge issue for marriages, and the financial times we are currently enduring have taken their toll on many families. But we can take control of this area of our marriages and make it what it needs to be. When we make the choice to keep spending under control, everyone benefits, including our children.

Discussion Group Questions

1. Brainstorm some ways to save money.

2. What is your biggest issue with money? What is your greatest victory?

3. Just an idea—ya'll are coming to the end of this book. Maybe you could take a financial class together?

Chapter 10:

Little Future Cops

Our three boys grew up knowing the risks. We never lied to them about it, but it wasn't what we talked about at the dinner table either. But what they also knew was that if Mom or Dad died doing the job, we'd go out with a sense of pride, purpose, and loving what it was we were doing.

Jeri, former CHP and wife of CHP[16]

I felt a little left out when my son became a patrolman. Suddenly he and my husband had their own little language and a camaraderie. When your kids go into law enforcement, it's a whole different ball game.

Cassandra, wife and mother of CHP officers

It was a beautiful day at the park. The Easter egg hunt was over, but not all the eggs were found, so the older kids were searching the deep grass. Hot dogs sizzled on the grill. A couple of the dads were marveling together at how well the day was going.

"The kids are so well-behaved. I think it's because we don't let them get out of hand. They know if they misbehave, we'll clobber them!" said one officer, laughing.

Heads nodded in agreement because we understood; most cops' kids are held to a pretty high standard. Their dads have seen what happens out there on the street, and they don't want their kids to become *customers*. Chances are that if someone else heard this conversation, they might get the wrong idea. With all of the confusion about parenting these days, there are mixed messages about what is acceptable and not acceptable. But law enforcement parents tend to lean toward a stricter standard.

What's It Like To Be a Cop's Kid?

Cops' kids generally don't get away with much. Police officers are trained to be able to tell when someone's lying and their kids all the more. There's also a network of information that gets around as well, especially in rural areas. If an officer's kid gets into trouble, there's a good chance he'll find out about it.

One tendency for law enforcement parents is the need to protect. Recently we had a situation with our nineteen-year-old daughter in that she and her girlfriends befriended a boy who was very handsome and likable. Because they met him at a church youth group, the assumption was made that he was a great guy, and one of the girls developed a dating relationship with him. Then Brent found out that the boy was going to court for stealing a car and had a prior for

Victoria M. Newman

marijuana possession. Oh, the tearful conversations we had to have with that one! We talked about boundaries with a person who engages in criminal activity even though likable and that it was a bad idea that he come to our home. She was convinced that he had changed his ways, yet Brent could tell from his excuses that he hadn't yet experienced a turnaround. Out of respect for Brent, our daughter made a choice to distance herself from him in their group and set boundaries like not driving him places. A couple of months later, he abruptly left the group to live on the streets in another state. Hurt that he left without a word, her friends suddenly realized that hanging out with this guy wasn't the smartest idea.

We can trust our husbands to protect our kids. But sometimes it can go too far. I had a conversation recently with an officer who'd seen a lot of death on duty. I asked him how he dealt with it. He told me that it manifested itself in being overprotective of his wife and kids. He has forbid them to go anywhere at times and won't allow people to drive them anywhere unless he first okays it. As you can imagine, this hasn't gone over well. Arguments ensued, and his wife thought he was being jealous. But that's not what it was. It was his inward responses to watching people die in his arms, guarding a little girl's dead body for hours to comfort a friend, and wiping another officer's blood off his uniform. It was these horrible images that manifested themselves into fear for his family.

These situations are so tricky because his fear is valid. The need to control is very real and possibly the only thing he can do to ensure the safety of his loved ones. But it's also problematic. The answer here is to recognize the reasons for the behavior and work from there to communicate. Your officer needs to be validated and respected in the process, and together you can move toward a workable solution.

Appearance may be a big deal to a police parent as well. Earrings, tattoos, baggy pants, and hairstyles matter to police officers. I've listened to several of our non-law enforcement friends talk about not making a big deal out of phases their kids go through. But police officers make judgments every shift about people they deal with on the street. Their lives can depend on it. They are looking for signs of criminal behavior and if the individual has a weapon. There are clues they look for in clothing and behavior, and some of these same clues may appeal to our own kids at some point. But law enforcement parents just don't want their kids even remotely resembling the people they put in jail.

Mom and Dad: United Front

So, what if you have a different parenting philosophy than your husband? What if you don't match up on the expectations of your children? Who determines what the rules will be?

Both of you do. If the two of you have different standards of behavior for your kids, nobody wins. Your

Victoria M. Newman

kids will be confused for awhile, and then they'll figure it out and be very smart. They will parent shop and inadvertently pit the two of you against each other. At that point it becomes a real mess. But if you and your husband have different viewpoints, you'll do yourself a favor to unify.

Start with things you both want your children to embrace. Morals. Values. Education. Faith. The big things you both want to instill in your children. Then work from there. Look for positive ways to teach them, such as spending time and actually talking about values. When situations arise you can use them as teaching moments. How you conduct yourself in the home and with others is also instilling your values in them as they watch you. Ask yourselves, "Where are the boundaries?" and "What are the consequences of crossing those boundaries?"

Brad and Heidi valued truthfulness in their kids. They felt that if they could trust what their children said, then they could build core values on that trust. Because kids are tempted to lie, they came up with a serious consequence: it was Tabasco sauce on the tongue. Fully edible and harmless, it brought temporary pain. It was a powerful deterrent for their children, a lesson that lies cause real pain. They didn't have much trouble with their kids telling the truth after that.

Children need to know where the boundaries are and the consequences of wandering outside those boundaries. Most law enforcement parents understand this because they administer the consequences of those who don't have boundaries every shift. But here's the key: children who have lovingly been given the perimeters for behavior and firm follow up to help them rely on those boundaries feel secure. It doesn't mean they won't try to push the limits. But it gives them peace, knowing that they have room to grow and be kids within the safety of balanced behavior. These perimeters also give the child a sense of dignity.

A couple of years ago, Brent and I had an issue with one of our teenagers. There was a breakdown in trust as boundaries were broken. For the first time, we found ourselves with different views on how to handle things. Brent took an aggressive approach, and I preferred to be more passive, seeing our child's point of view. Both of us loved our child fiercely, but we had differences in how to respond. As the months passed and things began to improve, I realized I had taken sides with my teenager. This wasn't wise. I could see both sides, but because I didn't align myself completely with my husband, I caused more harm to their relationship and ours. Brent didn't feel supported, and I think our child lost some respect for me in the process. But it's never too late; we talked it out and realized there were more similarities than differences that we could agree and act on. The most important thing was to be unified as parents.

When you and your husband set the boundaries for your kids, respect his instincts. It's always better to set the bar a little higher and adjust later if needed as you both grow in your parenting. Giving more privileges

Victoria M. Newman

up front and then taking them back later causes a lot of frustration in your kids.

Kid Communication

Kendra's six-year-old son knew Daddy went to work to arrest bad guys. Diedra and her husband sat their boys down at the ages of twelve and ten and had a heart to heart about what Dad's job entailed. Betty's eight- and nine-year-old kids watched their daddy on television during a standoff. I have been asked over and over, what are the guidelines for letting our kids know what their daddy does? How much information is okay and when?

As I've thought about this question, I've realized that there's no right answer. It really depends on the relationship you have with your kids, and what you think they can handle at what age. I don't remember ever sitting our children down to have a heart to heart about Daddy's job. If they had questions, we provided an age-appropriate response. We didn't offer more than what we thought they could handle at the time but made sure we answered their questions truthfully. I don't remember our kids ever fearing for their dad's safety on duty. I think this is because Brent and I never made it a habit to worry about what could happen, and they took their cues from us.

I do know that our kids suffered disappointment when Brent wasn't there for sports games, Fourth of July fireworks, and other things that came up here and there. Over the years he's tried to make as many events as he can, but there were times he just couldn't be there. But if there was something important that he couldn't make it to, we always tried to make up for it later.

When Brent was commuting to the Bay Area during the week and home on weekends only, he had to miss many kid events. Our youngest daughter was in a program through our church in which she conquered challenges weekly and received promotions in return, using a medieval theme as the backdrop. They had really great ceremonies where the child would be honored for their accomplishment. But the ceremony was on a Wednesday night. She was really sad that Dad was gone. We told her that although he wouldn't be able to be there, we would tape it so he could see it later. What we didn't tell her was that Brent worked out his schedule and drove back that night, arriving just in time. The look on her face when she saw him was priceless. She burst into big, happy tears and ran to hug him really tightly.

With a little planning and creativity, we can redeem the events our husbands miss. As moms, we have to lower the expectations of our kids when the career calls. But when we take the time to make special efforts to make memories, it makes up for it. In fact, these are some of the best days of their lives.

Victoria M. Newman

Gun Safety

When our oldest son was little, we got a kick out of the way he tied his cuddle blanket around his neck, made guns out of whatever was around, and ran off to fight the bad guys. When Brent's leather holders for badges and guns were retired, our son appointed himself heir to them. Then as he got older, it was Nerf guns and laser tag. At times our home was converted into a war zone, with the screens taken out of the windows, the lights out, and sweaty boys hiding, shooting foam darts at each other, and leaping in and out of the house through the windows—serious fun. Finally he progressed to Air Soft guns and paintball as a teenager. He and his buddies found empty fields with lots of bushes, trees, and ditches and got down and dirty, strategizing all the way. I think he even borrowed some of Brent's old Kevlar panels and eye gear to protect himself from welts.

As you can see, we have a relaxed view of guns in our family. But that doesn't mean we don't take gun safety seriously. When Brent brings his duty weapon home, he keeps it secure and teaches the kids about how the gun works and the correct way to handle it. He also cleans his weapon at work. There is an attitude of respect, not making a big deal out of it, but rather stressing the importance of keeping it pointed away from everyone even when it is unable to fire. The kids know that they are never to handle it by themselves and under no circumstances with another child. This would never happen anyway; Brent keeps his gun with him and will leave it in his locker at work more often than not.

If your home has other weapons, though, it is imperative that you get a safe that is childproof. We all know of a tragic story or two where accidents have happened. Kids can be unpredictable even when we train them. Talk with your kids about guns at friends' homes as well or if someone brings a weapon to school. They may respect your rules at home, but their curiosity may get the best of them somewhere else. We also use news of gun accidents to remind them of what to do in these situations.

Guns aren't the only thing we need to think about. Kids also need to understand that they don't want to get into the pepper spray, Taser gun, or the handcuffs. One afternoon Brent laid his gun belt on the bed right beside me, and our youngest son asked to see the handcuffs. Brent got them out and gave them to him. But before we could say anything, he put them on himself and started laughing. Until he realized that Brent's handcuff keys were at the office, forty minutes away! It took some rummaging through the junk drawers and a call to a cop neighbor before we finally found an extra key. Our son doesn't go near the handcuffs anymore. Sometimes natural consequences cure whatever foolishness our kids dish up.

Victoria M. Newman

Dads Need Their Kids

When Brent became a highway patrolman, I was the one who comforted him when he came home. But after we started having children, I noticed a little shift. It seemed to me that he was more excited to see them than me when he came home. I used to get a little jealous, but then I decided to grow up.

I've come to understand that my husband needs and feeds off of his kids. He needs their optimism. He needs their innocence. He sees in them that there is good in the world, and it's worth fighting for. I know that may sound a little dramatic, but it's true. He may not even realize it. But coming home and holding his baby girl or wrestling on the floor with his boys—my husband needs this. Chances are so does yours.

Almost every day, year after year, there has been a wrestling session at our home. It started when our oldest daughter could crawl. Brent tackled her—lovingly, of course—and she would laugh until her belly hurt. It's continued through the years, and now we have to clear a large space, as the legs and arms are much longer, but the laughter still rings through the halls. I call it wrestle therapy, and Brent needs it just as much as the kids.

But I've always been the stick in the mud. I'm the one who's moving the vase or scolding when it gets too rough. And they laugh at me and sometimes pull me in against my will. Usually it ends with my stomach aching because I can't stop laughing. So, let them wrestle. Let them throw footballs (soft ones) in at least one room of the house. Let them cuddle past bedtime. It is good for our husbands' souls, and it helps to balance out the harder parts of his job. The kids love it too.

On the Other Hand...

There are other seasons in a law enforcement career that aren't so great for kids. Sometimes your husband will need some quiet, alone time. When he's had a really bad day, he might not be able to handle the chaos that kids create. Several of my law enforcement friends have told me that they have had to take the kids somewhere else or send their husbands to the gym. Being quick to anger, irritable, or just in his own little world is a reality at some point. Unfortunately this can be really hurtful to the children who don't understand.

That's where we come in. Our husbands need a little space, exercise, time, or sleep to get back on track. We can create room for this, depending on our creativity and our attitudes. If we're full of resentment, our kids will pick up on it and be resentful. If we are patient, our kids will try to be patient. If we give him a little room for moods, it won't be so traumatic for the kids. Then, when he's calmed down a bit, you and the kids can engage him in the family goings on.

It's important to communicate to your kids, no matter what the age, what is going on. For little ones you can tell them that Daddy's had a bad day, and he needs some time to deal with it. For older kids you can give a little more detail, as appropriate. But the

Victoria M. Newman

attitude is support and love, not condemnation. We all have moods from time to time, and home is the best place to work through them, especially if we give each other the space to do it.

A CHiP Off the Ol' Block

I felt like I'd just been socked in the gut. I had the phone in my ear, and my son had just announced he needed his birth certificate ASAP, as he was joining the Marines. Oof. It came out of left field and reduced me to tears.

Now, you have to understand something. I've been a law enforcement wife for over twenty years. I've dealt with the risks and realities of what that means. But it's different when it's your baby.

My friend Brenna agrees wholeheartedly. Things were vastly different when her sons joined the highway patrol as opposed to her husband. "My husband was a man, but I still look at my boys as my children. It's very different with your kids. I'm proud of them. I think it's a great career, but it's hard to see them out there on the road."

So, what's a mom to do when her babies grow up and follow in their Dad's footsteps?

As I've interviewed a couple of my friends who are in this situation, I've come up with a few ideas. Ideas that I will be using if my son is deployed or if any of my kids choose police work.

- If it's fear you're feeling, deal with it head on. Go back to chapter six and reread with your kids in mind.

- Let go. If your child is going into this line of work, he/she's an adult. If you're struggling and you have a close relationship, maybe you could line up some phone calls to get you acclimated. Brenna did this. She had her son call her when he got home after every shift for the first couple months. He was willing to do this for her, and she eventually made peace within herself. She's now letting go, and he's doing well as a young officer.

- Be there for your child's spouse. Remember that this is all new to them, and you could be a great resource for talking things through. Make yourself available, but don't interfere.

- Enjoy the interaction between your husband and your child. There will be a new bond there that is enjoyable to watch. It's satisfying to see your child grow up and follow in the family way. Support, love, and enjoy.

The Greatest Gift

Finally, the best way to support your kids and your family as a unit is to build a good marriage. Your kids thrive when you and your husband are working together, giving each other support through good times and bad.

Victoria M. Newman

They are learning the positive value of loving in all circumstances. It doesn't have to be perfect. Just real.

Discussion Group Questions

1.   Are you a daughter of a police officer? If so, describe your memories and how they affected you.

2.   Talk about some ways to create memories with children and Daddy amidst his schedule.

3.   Talk about how your husband needs his kids. Do you agree with this? Have you noticed this in your own family?

4.   Put together an event that is especially for the kids. Get your husbands involved in the planning.

Chapter 11:

To Serve and Protect (Your Marriage, That Is!)

Marriage is an armed alliance against the outside world.

Gilbert Keith Chesterson

Being a good husband is like being a gardener. You've got to give your partner lots of water and sunshine (love and support).

Jack Black

In October 2010, the Pew Research Center came out with a survey that claimed four out of ten American adults feel that marriage is becoming obsolete.[17] That's alarming, considering that marriage/family is the foundational unit for society as a whole. There are many assaults on marriages these days—outside pressures, inward hurts, past baggage, other relationships (in-laws, exes, adultery), and an overall lack of marital know how. They threaten the overall well being of two people who have committed their lives to one another as well as the children involved.

But our marriages are worth fighting for.

Just like our husbands take an oath to serve and protect the public from lawlessness and to preserve the peace no matter the cost, we can choose to serve and protect our marriages as well. The following is an adaptation from a Texas police officer's oath that I found online.[18] What if we each took an oath that looks like this:

As a partner in this marriage, my fundamental duty is to serve my spouse; to safeguard our union; to protect our commitment against those who would seek to destroy it, and to respect the person to whom I'm bound in liberty, equality, and love.

I will keep myself unsullied as an example to my children; maintain courageous calm in the face of conflict and difficult circumstances; develop self-restraint; and be constantly mindful of the welfare of my family. Honest in thought and deed within my marriage, I will be exemplary in keeping myself only to my spouse. Whatever I see or hear in a confidential nature or that my spouse confides in me will be kept ever secret unless given permission to share with others.

I will never act unbecomingly or permit feelings of animosity and unforgiveness to influence my decisions in this marriage. With no compromise and relentless tenacity, I will devote myself to my spouse courteously and

Victoria M. Newman

appropriately without fear, malice or ill will, never employing unnecessary force or violence.

I recognize the ring on my finger as a symbol of commitment, and I accept it as a sacred trust to be held so long as I live. I will constantly strive to achieve these objectives and ideals, dedicating myself before God to my chosen partner... my spouse.

As cop wives, we have committed ourselves to lay down certain rights of ours for the greater good of our country, state, county, or city. It takes courage, determination, and unselfishness to see this through. Likewise, we must pledge to do the same with each other, to ensure our marriages are healthy and thriving for the duration of our lives together. And it doesn't require anything less than the same attitudes mentioned above. We must serve and protect our marriages much like officers serve and protect the population.

Serve Your Marriage Well: Build Trust

To have a thriving relationship we must have trust. Trust is a "firm belief or confidence in the honesty, integrity, reliability, justice, etc. of another person or thing."[19] When Brent and I started dating each other, we had guarded trust. We didn't know each other yet. Then over time that confidence grew through experience and as we learned more about each other's character. At some point, you and I made commitments and pledged vows at our weddings to honor those commitments. These were formal declarations of trust in each other, our firm belief that our spouses will follow through on their word.

One of the main reasons I chose Brent to share my life with is that I saw that he had integrity. He was loyal and did what he said he would do. This was incredibly important to me because in my dating experience this was very hard to find. Relationship after relationship ended because of another girl entering the picture; they simply found someone better. This left me with a couple of problems. First, the hurt ran deep. It surfaced in unattractive ways like jealousy and suspicion. Second, I didn't trust men. But Brent was very different from the other guys I had dated. He seemed trustworthy, so I decided to take a chance one last time.

I wish I could say it was easy to build trust in Brent. But it wasn't. Not because of anything he did or didn't do but because inwardly I was programmed to expect he would, at some point, leave me for someone else. It was my feeble protection from getting hurt. But, in spite of my trust issues, he has been faithful to me for over twenty-three years now. Building trust, or confidence, in his character and our relationship has been a slow but sure process as we navigate through life together. I have put him through a lot, but he's been very patient with me, reassuring me and loving me in the midst of my shortcomings. It's been a tough but beautiful transformation as we build trust together.

Deposits into the Trust Account

Building trust in your relationship takes a lifetime. As the years progress, there will be deposits and withdrawals as we rise and fall to each other's expectations. I mentioned this in chapter four. Much like a bank account, we give and take from our relationships. Here are some ways to invest in our marriages.

Time Is Not a Luxury

We need to spend time together alone. This is a no brainer, right? Perhaps when relationships are young the thought of not spending time together is ludicrous. But when kids are added to the mix, careers take more time than usual, and responsibilities pile up; believe me, spending time together can seem like a luxury. But it isn't a luxury. It's a need, and as all these other things crowd our lives, we need time together all the more. This is when we have to get creative and *intentional*.

We need this time to get in sync with one another. As we grow older, we undergo changes good and difficult. We need to dream together about the future no matter how long we've been married. We need to talk about things we enjoy individually and together. We need to laugh together. We need to set financial goals. We need to share a vision for our kids. All of this requires time to talk through. Whether we've been married three years or thirty, these conversations are crucial to us as individuals and as couples.

Four Levels of Communication

We must learn to explore all four levels of communication that we employ. The first is housekeeping. This is the everyday talking of who's picking up the kids or "I'll be working an overtime detail this Friday." The second level is sharing what happened in the course of the day while we're apart. For police officers this may require a different level of trust in his wife than non-law enforcement because of the potential gravity of what has actually happened in his day. Building trust at this level means that the response be appropriate. If an officer shares with his wife that he watched a man die on duty, her ability to handle that information actually increases or decreases his trust in her. Because of this the third level may be intimately related. The third level is when we share parts of ourselves, responses to the goings on of the day. Hopes and fears come out at this level and, depending on each others' responses, lay the groundwork for the deep conversations.

Mike and Trina have been married thirty-two years, and he is newly retired from law enforcement. When Trina recently brought home an issue she was really bothered about, Mike quickly came up with a solution. This wasn't the response Trina was looking for. Instantly there was conflict. She wasn't coming to him with a problem that needed solving but rather for him to be quiet and let her process it through. As an officer Mike was there to fix the problem. At home he needed a different, more delicate approach.

Victoria M. Newman

The last level of communication springs from an appropriate, trusted response to level three. As Mike listens to Trina, asking clarifying questions and being patient while she processes it through, something incredible happens. Intimacy. There is a soul-to-soul connection that says, "I'm safe. You can trust me with your vulnerabilities." When we learn to respond to each other out of love, the protective layers of self-preservation come off, and we can share pieces of who we are without fear. We can communicate on a soul-to-soul level.

As we move through the four levels of communication, we build trust in each other as we engage. As you make deposits of time and choose to listen in a way that feels safe to your partner, you can get to that soul-to-soul level.

Keep Your Word

We need to keep our word. Believe it or not, sometimes this can be difficult for law enforcement marriages. Not that we lie, for we generally place great value on truth. It's more than this. It's about follow through. Life in law enforcement can be one promise unkept after another. With a crisis-driven career and a sincere love for it, sometimes an officer can't (or won't) always live up to what he promises. Many officers' wives harden because too many promises go unmet and wound her. After awhile she will develop protections against getting hurt again, and that will show up as frustration, sarcasm, and disrespect. She doesn't trust anymore.

This is not just about cops. It's universal. If you promise to call your mother, call your mother. If you say you'll pay the water bill, pay it on time. If you resolve to go on a vacation for the first time in two years, make choices that will allow it to happen. Focused follow up is crucial to build trust.

Build Each Other Up

Fourth, build each other up. We all need encouragement, some more than others. As we grow closer to our spouses, we will learn the most effective ways of building each other up and, unfortunately, tearing down. With some, encouragement comes through words. With others, it's respect. Still others, it's cooking them a good meal.

Nothing makes us more unsafe than when we tear down other people with our actions and words. Your comfort level of straight talk will depend upon the way your own family communicated with each other. If you come from a family of cops, chances are you can take it head on. If you come from a more sensitive family, you may get hurt easily. My family was the type to just let it go and not talk about the hard stuff. It took me a long time to be able to communicate delicate issues without feeling attacked or that I was wounding someone else. When Brent gave me permission to express my frustration with him verbally, we built trust.

Victoria M. Newman

Get Real

Be real. I read an interview with actor Jack Black in which he talks about marriage. "I have a tendency to do whatever my wife wants," he confides, "and then anger builds up inside me and comes out in little passive-aggressive bursts. It's better to just communicate your desires up front from the get-go."[20] How many times do we play this game? Either we don't know how we feel about things, or we just don't want to deal with the issue at hand. Instead, we don't communicate and then let drama develop.

Brianna felt this way about her husband, Mark, when he was working a lot of hours on the road. "I was just too demanding. I wanted him home. I would get upset," she admits, "I would never really come out and say that, but it came out in other ways. Cold shoulder, rude. I would be upset, and he wouldn't even know why."

Oh, ladies, we are so good at this! I used to put Brent through this all the time. He had to work to get my true feelings out of me. It was a little game I played, and, boy, did it get old after a couple of years. I'm glad to say that I have learned to be real the first time. I am only able to do this because my husband and I have built up trust over the years.

Lastly, nurture intimacy. Oh, yes, we have to go *there*. Sex, the ultimate intimate act, definitely builds trust. And if there are issues with sex, it can tear trust apart.

A Few Words about Sex...

Every time I get women together to talk about marriage, inevitably the conversation will veer toward sex. In fact, when I had a group of newlywed wives over to talk about several aspects of marriage, I couldn't get them to talk about anything else! For hours we delved into the subject of marital sex amidst giggles and tears. There are always questions, there are always hurts, and there is always some confusion.

I know of three marriages just off the top of my head in which the wife stopped having sex with her husband. Two ended in divorce, and the jury is still out on the third (not looking good). If you are married and healthy but are not having sex regularly, there is an underlying problem that needs to be addressed.

Sex is a beautiful experience that creates intimacy within committed love. It literally brings two people together and makes them one. There is no other act that is as binding, no other act that is as pleasurable, and no other act that is so vulnerable. When we have sex, we are inviting our spouse into our most private places, giving and taking of ourselves in an incredibly intimate way. At that point there is nothing between us. Healthy sex between a married couple builds trust.

So why are so many couples struggling in this area? Why are husbands and wives withholding themselves from each other? And why does it seem like we don't want to have sex after we're married when we couldn't keep our hands off each other before? I'm not an expert, but based on many conversations over the years, I've

Victoria M. Newman

come up with five circumstances that affect our sexual relationships as married couples.

The first circumstance relates to our husbands' schedules. Shift work can be really difficult on the frequency of sex. Mandy and George both worked for government agencies. She worked the day shift in an office, and he worked graveyards in the jail. For the first three years of their marriage, they literally passed each other on the freeway coming and going to work. They rarely shared a bed together. However, they got creative and made it work, even becoming pregnant during that time!

The second circumstance has to do with the seasons we go through over the years. As newlyweds, we are adventurous and eager, but then when small children start filling the home, the quantity of sex tends to wane. Young moms have so many demands—little ones hanging on them and needing constant attention. They are always tired. It's hard to feel sexy when Mom is sporting extra baby weight and wearing dirty T-shirts all the time. When Marlo suggests a little tryst in the bedroom in the middle of the day, Erica tries to comply. But she says, "Shifting from diapers to sex is difficult for me. I'm willing to take one for the team, but I need more time to enjoy this!"

As kids grow older, there seems to be a little more desire for sex. Susan and her husband, Jason, have three school-age boys. When a few of us brought up the fact that it's hard to find the time to have sex, her response was, "It doesn't take long, people! Sometimes we just head for the laundry room and lock ourselves in for a quickie!" After young adult kids leave the house, I've heard several friends comment that they feel like new-lyweds again, having sex wherever and whenever just because they can!

The third circumstance is stress. When we deal with heavy stuff and our lives become difficult, sex seems to take a back seat. However, this is when we may have to be proactive, choosing to have sex together. Nancy calls this "mercy sex." She understands that her husband, Tom, needs to have sex frequently. She doesn't need it as often, and it requires some sacrifice on her part, especially when she's had a stressful day at work or with her three boys. But she willingly and cheerfully engages in mercy sex with her husband out of love for him. In stressful times the desires may not be there because we're distracted, but when we make the effort to please each other, it seems to relieve some of that pent up tension. And it builds trust.

The last two circumstances are a little more difficult to overcome. The first is past baggage. It is possible that one of you may have suffered pain because of sex. Abuse, molestation, or past relationships that bring painful memories back may be the reason for disinterest in sex. Sex between a married couple is a positive thing, but if sex is a negative in your mind because of a painful experience, you may not be able to get there. In her book *Kiss Me Again – Restoring Lost Intimacy in Marriage* Barbara Wilson says,

Victoria M. Newman

Rape or abuse is a big deal. If this is your story, please understand it wasn't your fault. Even so, you will not "get over it" on your own. Until you have healing, sex with your husband will continue to trigger negative emotions, including shame, that will prevent you from being able to trust him and be vulnerable with him emotionally and physically. The lack of trust and emotional intimacy will diminish your enjoyment of and desire for sex.[21]

If this is the case for you, you need healing. Talk together about this; many times a couple can work through it with the help of a counselor. I know several women who have suffered rape and child abuse. After their journeys of healing, they found hope as their emotional and sexual relationships with their husbands improved.

The last circumstance is one you may not have heard of. It's sexual bonding from past relationships. The idea is that each time you have sex with a partner, you bond with that person physically, emotionally, and physiologically. I again refer to Barbara Wilson:

Scientists have discovered that in addition to releasing chemicals [endorphins and enkephalins] during sex, the brain also releases a hormone called oxytocin, and these work together to create a strong bond between people. This invisible bond works like superglue, permanently attaching us emotionally and spiritually to a lover. This bonding happens with everyone with whom we have sex—whether we're married or single, and whether the sex is consensual or forced. The past ten years have produced cutting-edge research on this hormone, which scientists have dubbed the hormone of love.[22]

This powerful hormone of love is designed to keep us bonded for a lifetime. But if we have had past sexual relationships, this also happened with each person we had sex with. Can you see how this could be an issue? If we have been bonded with someone sexually, break away from them, then repeat the process again (and again), this can leave us broken and racked with emotional pain. Another problem is this hormone of love decreases with each partner. This explains why some people can have casual, non-committed sex with multiple partners. If you or your husband are experiencing a lack of desire, it could be that you have bonded with other people intimately, and it's affecting the sexual relationship you now have with your spouse.

There is hope here though. You can break these bonds and get healing. But it's a process that requires much more explanation. If this is something that rings familiar, you may want to pick up the book I referred to earlier. See the resources section at the back of this book.

Victoria M. Newman

Withdrawals from the Trust Account

When we are building trust in our marriages, unfortunately there will be some things that will cause us to mistrust. None of us married a perfect person; perfect people only exist in fairy tales. Inevitably we will let each other down. Expecting this from the get-go, we may be able to let things slide here and there, but there are things we do that negatively affect trust.

The first is comparisons. Even though we are married, most of us lead different lives while we are apart. Because officers are dealing with life and death, we can make assumptions that he will have the tougher job. But that doesn't mean that taking care of the kids at home isn't stressful too. Or working at the bank. Or volunteering at the community center. However we spend our time, there will be stress as well. This came up at my cop wives' gathering.

Melissa is new to this whole journey. Her husband has been a patrolman for only two years, but was a Marine before that. She shared that her biggest struggle is when she has an issue, her husband minimizes it. "He says, 'What's the big deal? Get over it! So she said this and that! Who cares?' He thinks my world is so small and insignificant. But I'm like, 'It's my world. I listen to all of your [stories] on duty, why can't you just listen to my world? Can't you just *pretend* to care?'"

Ellen chimed in with, "My husband does this too. He says, 'Ooh, catastrophe! Both the PTA *and* this other conflict? Oh my gosh!' I know that in the overall scheme of things, I will never out trump him. But it's important to me. So I just call my friend because she cares. And she'll remind me how much I love him. She says, 'I know he's crazy, but he loves you!'"

Comparing ourselves to one another separates. Perhaps in wanting understanding from one another, we inadvertently alienate the other spouse. Someone comes away devalued because the comparison ends in a place where someone has it better (or worse). More often than not, someone comes away with the feeling that their issue doesn't matter because it's not as bad as their spouse's issue. In Ellen's case it shuts down communication altogether, leaving some doubt in her mind that her husband loves her.

The second withdrawal from the trust account is trying to control each other. This is very common in law enforcement marriages. Usually the person who is trying to control the other doesn't mean to hurt anyone. It tends to be a reflection of selfishness and/or fear. Fear of the what if. Fear of my inability to handle whatever the situation is. Fear of trusting. Yes, I said that right. When we try to control another human being, we are, in essence, saying that we don't trust them. *I need to take control because you are inadequate.* Ouch. Selfishness comes in when we assume that we have to take control because we feel we are superior in our ability: *I'm better equipped than you.* Manipulation can be a result of this as well. *I want something, and I don't trust you enough to just ask for it. I need to get it by fooling you or wearing you down by making you angry.* Do you understand how this can break down trust?

Victoria M. Newman

The third withdrawal is the most obvious: lying. When we intentionally lead others to believe something other than what is the truth, we lie. There are big lies and small lies in regards to the impact that the lie will have. But they are still lies, and they break down trust.

Most of us lie because we have fallen short in some way and we are too embarrassed to own up to it. We are protecting our pride. Some of us lie to keep from getting caught in something we've done wrong. We are protecting our deceit. Some of us lie because we just don't like the truth.

The last withdrawal is the big one: having an extra-marital affair. This is the ultimate breech of trust in a marriage and more often than not will break the marriage apart. Someone brings another person into your union, and that person obviously isn't welcome by the spouse. Unfortunately, this happens often, but we can safeguard our marriages against it. We just have to set some boundaries.

Protect Your Marriage: Set Boundaries

In the last chapter I talked about boundaries for our kids. I mentioned that these boundaries keep them safe, secure, and they protect their dignity. It is the same for us in our marriage. We too need boundaries to keep our marriage safe, secure, and to protect our dignity as a couple.

Donna has a philosophy about boundaries. She is a very self-assured woman and has survived her husband's twenty-nine-year career in law enforcement intact and with strong beliefs. When I asked her to share with me something that helped her in her marriage, she told me that they set boundaries. It was what helped her maneuver through both of their careers, children, household, etc. She said they first established boundaries. Then they learned to communicate those boundaries. And finally they enforced the boundaries. In Donna's case, she was very aware of what she could and couldn't handle. So she divvyed up responsibilities for the household and then kept everyone accountable. Chores, communication, events, behavior—the expectations were communicated and, for the most part, adhered to.

As our marriages progress in trust and communication, we will learn what each other can handle and what will become an issue. This applies to all aspects of our lives—children, work, family interaction, etc., and thus there will be boundaries that will be made by accident. Boundaries made by accident are usually touchy subjects that we don't want to talk about because they invoke emotion. Some examples are "We never lean against Dad's car," or "We never talk about overeating in our family." But as we intentionally put in perimeters to safeguard our marriages, we need to actually talk about establishing them and why, communicating about them freely, and thus enforcing them in our lives.

Victoria M. Newman

The boundaries that we need to instill in our marriages intentionally are those that protect three areas of vulnerability: our minds and emotions, our bodies, and our unions.

Guard Your Mind/Emotions

Actions come from choices. Choices come from mindsets. Therefore we have to start with our minds. Our minds are the key to keeping our emotions in check.

Most extramarital affairs begin with some kind of emotional attraction. This is especially the case for women. Emotional affairs can and do lead to sexual affairs. It usually starts out innocent. There's a mutual respect that leads to more time together. The respect can lead to trust, and, if not checked, vulnerability and dependence develops. This is called an emotional affair. We begin to depend on someone other than our spouse for emotional support, and this is dangerous.

This type of thing happened in the aftermath of 9/11. Because so many policemen and firemen were lost, those who survived decided that they would take care of the surviving families. In many cases emotional affairs began as the widows depended emotionally upon these men. The emotional affairs developed into sexual relationships, and some of these men divorced their wives and married the widows. It was devastating on many levels, as wives and children of surviving rescuers eventually lost them to the widows of those who had died. They too became victims of 9/11.

So how do we protect ourselves from emotional affairs? First of all awareness helps. Beware the person who claims that you are the only one who they can talk to. This is a red flag because it isn't true. What is true is that this person has chosen you as their confidant and is already emotionally attached. Run—don't walk—to the nearest exit!

Create boundaries with others in this regard. Learn to keep an eye out for those who would seek to attach themselves emotionally to you. Brent refers to his "Spidey-sense," a feeling that something isn't quite right that puts his guard up even if he can't identify it at a conscious level.

If you find yourself attracted to someone else and really enjoy a connection on an emotional level, distance yourself immediately. Then go the extra mile. Talk about it with a close friend. I have found that any danger lurking in the shadows will disappear when the light is turned on. I have sought accountability from a few close friends who know my husband and love him. I gave them permission to look me in the eye and ask me about attractions. It keeps me accountable.

One last thing. If your emotional needs are being met by your spouse, the temptation to connect with another man is decreased.

Guard Your Body

Every affair begins with a choice to entertain temptations. Our bodies have strong biological needs. Some-

Victoria M. Newman

how those needs have to be met. So the first way to safeguard yourself from extramarital affairs is to have frequent sex together. Like I said earlier, sometimes this will take an act of the will, depending on circumstances. But if you are investing in your sex life, temptations toward someone else will naturally decrease.

But what if one of you is in a season of dryness in this area? What if you aren't getting along like you used to? What if our eyes wander toward someone who is attractive? How can we abstain from these temptations when there are problems at home?

We have to be all the more intentional. All the more vigilant. Recognize the enemies that want to destroy our marriage, and be wise to our own vulnerabilities.

Many years ago I went on a trip with my husband. We attended a retirement dinner and then met with some friends at a little club nearby. As we visited, another man joined us. Everyone knew him but me, but I noticed he was very handsome. After we'd been there for awhile, the band started playing these great, older songs. The man started dancing with other ladies at the table and then asked me. Brent, who hates to dance, told me to go ahead. So I did. I danced with this man for several songs, returned to my husband, and that was that. Until he kept creeping into my thoughts.

As I talked this out with a girlfriend, she told me that I needed to watch myself with the dancing. She was right. I realized that dancing was a temptation trigger for me. I resolved to only dance with my husband from then on. We need to understand what turns us on and then reserve that trigger for our spouse. I later shared this with Brent, and, turns out, he is trying to develop a like for dancing because he loves me!

Another way to safeguard ourselves from adultery is to keep away from the wrong places and the wrong people. I call these danger zones. If someone is coming on to you, cut off contact with them. If your friends are getting wild in Las Vegas, volunteer to be the designated driver or the one who makes sure they don't regret something in the morning. You'll thank yourself later on.

If you are attracted to someone else, make yourself accountable to someone you trust. And that could include your own spouse.

Guard Your Union

I once heard a speaker refer to sex as fire. He said, "A fire in the fireplace will warm a home. Fire outside of the fireplace will burn the house down." In other words, sex has great rewards if it has boundaries. Sex without boundaries can ruin everything. What do I mean by this?

I'm not talking about squashing your creativity in the bedroom. Sex is an intimate, trust-building uniting of two bodies, hearts, and souls. The boundary here is that we keep it just between husband and wife. We have to safeguard our union by not letting anything or anyone join us in the bedroom or come between us during sex. This includes other people. This includes

Victoria M. Newman

pornography. This includes letting our minds wander during sex. Any inclusion of others into our sexual relationship will break down the uniting factor in our relationship. And it will introduce mistrust.

The Perfect Storm

I have a friend I've known for almost thirty years. Recently Jill shared with me that she had an affair. After she peeled me off the floor from the shock (she was the last person I thought would do this), I asked her how it happened.

"It was the perfect storm," she said, "Kevin and I haven't been getting along. Our business was about to go under, we were arguing, we caught our boys smoking pot in the backyard… it seemed like everything in our lives was going wrong. At the same time, I found an old school acquaintance on Facebook. We were talking online, then started meeting together. He was the one thing in my life that brought happiness. We ended up in bed together."

At that point her life went from bad to worse. Their business went bankrupt, everyone was angry and hurt, and this didn't help their boys any. But she admitted it to her husband and took the consequences humbly. She didn't make excuses and apologized to several layers of family. It was touch and go for several months.

With the help of her family and close friends, she and her husband are rebuilding their marriage. They are slowly but surely retraining themselves to do things the right way. Rebuilding trust. Communicating. Choosing attitudes that build up instead of tear down. She is now accountable to friends and doesn't communicate on Facebook with old boyfriends anymore. Even after a serious breech of trust, Jill and Kevin have forgiven each other and are starting over. That takes character. That takes commitment.

What Do I Do if He Has an Affair?

We can try to do what we can to serve and protect our marriages, but sometimes things just go wrong. Infidelity happens, and tears at the very foundations of trust.

There are some cases in which the cop not only has an affair, but chooses to leave his family altogether. If this is your situation, my heart goes out to you. Your choice has been made for you, and you are left in shambles. I hope that you will seek healing in a safe place, with people who love you. At times like this, your support system will carry you forward while you grieve and rebuild.

There are other cases in which the affair happens, but the couple chooses to remain married. In most cases, there were problems before the affair occurred, and this is the event that wakes everybody up. They are devastated, but they choose to work through the grief together and make the changes necessary for a renewed marriage.

I have four girlfriends who have been victims of unfaithfulness; two of them are married to police

Victoria M. Newman

officers. Handsome husbands, nice guys, but they got caught up in waywardness. In talking with these gals over the years, I've made some observations that may be helpful should you find yourself in this predicament.

First, all four stayed with their husbands after the affair. I asked why. All said the same thing: their husbands were repentant. When they were caught, the husbands felt relief. They wanted their marriages back, and were willing not only to apologize, but to take the time necessary to prove their renewed love. This was the key for all four women.

All four took the chance to confront their husbands and communicate their hurt. This is very important for healing. When there is a hurt like this, it is imperative that the offending spouse understand that what they've done has damaged their partner, and their marriage. In three cases, there was also a confrontation via phone with the other woman. This seemed to help—it was a kind of reinsertion of their rightful place in their marriage. It also helped them to believe that the affair was indeed over. In the fourth case, my friend didn't want to go there.

All four women made a choice. They allowed themselves to grieve for a time, but then they chose to forgive. Forgiveness doesn't excuse the behavior, nor assert that what they did was okay. David Stoop, in his book *Forgiving the Unforgivable*, says that "Forgiving other people does not in any way benefit or let them off the hook. It allows us to cancel the debt they owe us, which in all probability they can never pay anyway.

We are the ones who are freed—from the expectation of restitution for the wrongs done to us."[23] I admire these ladies. It takes a lot of courage and character to choose to forgive.

Another observation is they surrounded themselves with those who supported their marriage. Trusted family, counselors, clergy, accountability partners, and close friends were crucial to the reconciliation process. These people loved them through the hurt, listened to their cries, and spoke truth into their marriages.

The last thing that all four of these gals did was go through the journey to rebuild trust. It wasn't easy, and it wasn't quick. In fact, they're still rebuilding. Their journeys have been two steps forward, one step back, again and again. But all four are on their way back to a better marriage than they had before.

Gratitude Goes a Long Way

The last thing that can protect your marriage is gratitude. When years run together and your marriage seems to take more work, it is easy to begin to lose perspective. We get tired. We get grumpy. And we can concentrate on each other's negative qualities and even be tempted to look elsewhere. Choosing to be grateful for each other can turn this around. We all have weaknesses and things in our character that could use improvement. But that's only half of the story. We all have good qualities, too. When we choose an attitude of thankfulness for positive things in our spouse, we

Victoria M. Newman

reinstate value to each other and our relationships. Gratitude protects.

Discussion Group Questions

1. What is one area of trust building you would like to see in your marriage?

2. What is one area of protection that you think your marriage needs?

Chapter 12:

A Seventy Year Vision

An excellent wife, who can find? For her worth is far above jewels. The heart of her husband trusts in her, and he will have no lack of gain.

Ancient Proverb

Love is spontaneous, but it has to be maintained by discipline.

Oswald Chambers

Being a cop's wife is tough. The title of this book explores the dichotomy of being a law enforcement spouse. On one hand, I must be strong—stubborn—even, in the pursuit of a lasting law enforcement marriage. But at the same time, he leans on me—looks to me for support. I'm his backup at home. I represent strength, yet gentleness.

We must fight for our marriages because of the nature of our husbands' jobs, yet we are careful to choose attitudes that soothe, encourage, and strengthen. We are advocates for our husbands, and there is no sitting on the sidelines. The life we chose with our officers is one that is lived out with character. We are tenacious fighters and gentle lovers.

As you process all that you've read within the pages of this book, I ask one final question. What is your vision for your marriage? What do you want your marriage to look like years from now? If you meander aimlessly from one year to the next, you'll get just that—time gone by that you can't account for. But if you want to have a marriage that is meaningful—you must take proactive steps toward that goal.

In February 2011, my grandparents celebrated their seventieth wedding anniversary. I love the old pictures of their young faces, polished and smiling, my grandma in her elegant 40's-style gown and my grandfather in his suit. They've been through the Depression, World War II, the Korean War, the Vietnam War, the Hippie Generation, the Cold War, the Kennedy Assassination, Martin Luther King, 9/11, the War on Terror, and the electronic revolution, among many other world events. Personally, they went through military deployment during wartime, several other careers, their son almost dying of a heart attack, the deaths of their parents, siblings and many friends, several homes in three states, weddings of descendents, divorces of descendents, serious health issues, sending grandchildren to war, and more good memories than they can recount. They have three children, nine grandchildren, four step-grandchildren, twenty-five great-grandchildren, one step-great-grandchild, and one great-great-grand-

Victoria M. Newman

child at the time of this writing. My grandpa says, "It's a little scary to see what all we've created!"

I recently asked my grandparents, "What's your secret? How have you stayed married all these years?"

My grandpa chuckled a bit and then said, "That's simple. God and a love between us." As the three of us talked, they elaborated a bit more, finishing each other's sentences like they have for many years. "When two people get married, you become one. When you're one, you have to stick together, or it doesn't work out! We also have had a lot of support from family, first from our parents, and now from you guys. We learned a lot of things over the years, and we tried to never make the same mistake twice. It's been a lot of little things that have all worked together."

Commitment. Flexibility. Communication. Mutual respect. Strong foundation. Support system. Perseverance. Trust. A lot of little things can work towards keeping a couple together—the same things I've written about here. But it isn't about just staying together—it's about building a good life together. One that defies statistics and thrives in the midst of difficulties.

It is possible to build a great law enforcement marriage. But this takes knowing what you want your marriage to be and then working at it day to day, year to year.

Like my grandparents, Brent and I look forward to growing old together. We want to love each other more deeply than we do today. We want to raise our kids to maturity in a safe and loving home, so that they, too, will raise great kids. It is this vision that spurs us on year after year.

I've talked a lot about different seasons throughout this book. At the time of this writing, Brent and I are on the brink of a new season. Our children are starting to head off into the world on their own. And as Brent's career grows more political with each promotion, we are learning to adapt to the challenges and rewards of leadership to those who drive the car and shoot the gun. As for me, I'm starting a new career as an author. It's all part of another rewarding adventure!

At some point, Brent's career as a highway patrol-man will come to an end. We will have a collection of awesome memories as we begin yet another season in our lives together, just the two of us. In the meantime, we'll keep at it, implementing what I've written on the pages of this book, and reinterpreting the principles to fit the circumstances we face year to year.

Marriage is hard for everyone. Marriage can be even harder for law enforcement. But you and your husband are a special and unique couple because you have willingly served the people in your jurisdiction and have pledged your best effort. You are noble and courageous. My hope and prayer for you both is that you will thrive through the seasons of your marriage in spite of the difficulties, perhaps one day celebrating seventy awesome years together.

Victoria M. Newman

Discussion Group Questions

1.   Identify an older married couple that you know who've done marriage well. What is one character trait you see in their relationship?

2.   What season are you in right now? How is that affecting your marriage?

3.   What is your vision for your marriage? Be specific.

4.   Put together a group date night with your husbands to celebrate your marriages. Make a toast to longevity!

Resources

Books

I Love a Cop, Ellen Kirschman, PhD

The Delicate Art of Dancing with Porcupines, Bob Phillips

The 5 Love Languages, Gary Chapman

Emotional Survival for Law Enforcement Officers, Kevin Gilmartin, PhD

Marital Intelligence – A Foolproof Guide to Saving and Strengthening Marriage, Gil Stieglitz

Caring Enough to Confront, David Augsburger

CopShock, Second Edition: Surviving Post-traumatic Stress Disorder (PTSD), Allen Kates

The Total Money Makeover, Dave Ramsay

Kiss Me Again – Restoring Lost Intimacy in Marriage, Barbara Wilson

My Life for Your Life, Clarke Paris

Websites

www.how2loveyourcop.com, Author's personal website

See author's website for updated links to other helpful sites for police wives.

Residential Retreats

West Coast Post-trauma Retreat, California

A five-day confidential program for first responders who are overwhelmed by job stress.
www.wcpr2001.org; (415)721-9789

On-Site Academy, Massachusetts

A three-day confidential program for first responders and military who are suffering from effects of their job.
www.onsiteacademy.org; (978) 874-0177

Endnotes

1   Ellen Kirschman, *I Love a Cop* (New York: The Guilford Press, 2007) Page 5.

2   Rudd, Johnathan. The FBI Law Enforcement Bulletin, September 2009

3   en.wikipedia.org/wiki/California_Highway_Patrol

4   Bob Phillips, *The Delicate Art of Dancing with Porcupines*, (Ventura, CA: Regal Books, 1989) page 43.

5   Kevin M. Gilmartin, *Emotional Survival for Law Enforcement*, (Tuscon, Arizona: E-S Press, 2002) page 50.

6   This statistic is based on population calculations.

7   Kevin Gilmartin, *Emotional Survival for Law Enforcement*, (Tuscon, Arizona: E-S Press, 2002) pages 89-90.

8   Correspondence, *Code 3 Magazine*, (Spring 2007).

9   www.money.cnn.com

10   Gil Stieglitz, *Marital Intelligence*, (Winona Lake, IN: BMH books, 2010) page 184.

11   Ellen Kirschman, *I Love a Cop* (New York: The Guilford Press, 2007) page 89.

12   David Augsburger, Caring Enough to Confront, (Ventura, CA: Regal Books, 2009) page 46-47.

13   David Augsburger, Caring Enough to Confront, (Ventura, CA: Regal Books, 2009) page 51.

14   http://www.copshock.com/description.php

15   Kevin Gilmartin, *Emotional Survival for Law Enforcement*, (Tuscon, Arizona: E-S Press, 2002) pages 128-129.

16   Correspondence, *Code 3 Magazine*, (Spring 2007).

17   http://today.msnbc.msn.com/id/40239472/ns/today-today_health/from/toolbar

18   http://answers.yahoo.com/question/index?qid=20080424104517AAJvlFj

19   Webster's New World College Dictionary

20 http://www.parade.com/celebrity/celebrity-parade/2010/1205-jack-black-gullivers-travels.html

21 Barbara Wilson, *Kiss Me Again*, (Colorado Springs, CO: Multnomah Books, 2009) page 22.

22 Barbara Wilson, *Kiss Me Again*, (Colorado Springs, CO: Multnomah Books, 2009) page 28-29.

23 David Stoop, *Forgiving the Unforgivable*, (Ventura, CA: Regal Books, 2005) page 34.

HOW TO LOVE YOUR COP WITH ATTITUDE